Praise for *The Teacher Leader*

"The authors provide an excellent basis for understanding the teacher leader. I'm confident that this book will provide a positive contribution to education." —**Dr. John W. Sparlin**, assistant superintendent for administrative services, School District 308, District Administration Center, Illinois

"In a time when the success of our children and schools is increasingly dependent on the combined efforts of the entire school family, teachers are called upon to provide more instructional and programmatic leadership than ever. This book should be required reading! The emphasis on core competencies combined with the clear and compelling examples make it practical as well as valuable. This book is thorough and helpful. I recommend it wholeheartedly!" —**Thomas P. Jandris**, PhD, senior vice president for innovation, dean, College of Graduate & Innovative Programs, Concordia University Chicago

"The role of the teacher leader is critical to the future of educational practice and this book is a practical and understandable resource. I highly recommend this book." —**Michael A. Jacoby**, EdD SFO, CAE, executive director, Illinois ASBO

"I recommend this book to all teachers and teacher leaders who want to excel in their vital roles. The authors have applied their vast experience and unparalleled knowledge and wisdom to develop this comprehensive volume on educational leadership!" —**Alan E. Meyer**, PhD interim president, Concordia University Chicago

"This book is not only a valuable resource for administrators who want to improve development of outstanding teacher leaders, but it can also be a resource for prospective teacher leaders." —**Mr. Kerry R. Leiby**, superintendent, Norridge School District 80, Illinois

"Drs. Tomal, Schilling, and Wilhite have provided not only a comprehensive framework for effective Teacher Leadership, they have also shared a wealth of resources, real-world applications and insights that any future leader or instructional coach would benefit from. This book won't simply sit on a shelf—it will serve as a guide to educational excellence." —**Michael Schlabra**, EdD, executive director for the division of research & doctoral programs associate, Concordia University Chicago

"Drs. Schilling, Tomal, and Wilhite have captured the 'essence of teacher leadership' that is well written and insightful. I highly recommend this book as a must read for leaders." —**Jon Mielke**, EdD, executive counselor for Christian education, and superintendent for The Lutheran Schools of Indiana

"Leadership is not a one-person job. In this well written, comprehensive book, the authors demonstrate our need for a model of shared leadership emerging today in schools called *The Teacher Leader*." —**Paul Sims**, PhD, associate professor, Concordia University Chicago

"In a time period of constant transitions in education, *The Teacher Leader*, by Drs. Tomal, Schilling, and Wilhite, uses practical methods of teacher leadership in the school setting for reaching new heights by utilizing effective change for student growth." —**Dr. James Rosborg**, director of master's in education, McKendree University

"The authors provide an excellent basis for understanding the teacher leader. This is especially important for individuals seeking to serve as teacher leaders." —**Sandra C. Coyner**, EdD, professor and interim chair, curricular and instructional studies, University of Akron, Ohio

"Finally a comprehensive blueprint of strategic competencies which will elevate teachers into teacher leaders as actors for change through their innate appreciation and understanding of the learning process, school improvement models, and risk taking. It establishes a new paradigm of leadership for school success." —**L. Arthur Safer**, PhD, associate professor, Concordia University Chicago

"This book integrates the key skills of an effective leader with the five domains of Emotional Intelligence that provides a comprehensive coverage of Teacher Leadership. It is a must read for all educators!" —**Dr. John Cindric, Jr.**, professor of leadership, organizational behavior & emotional intelligence, University of Findlay, Ohio

"This book provides focus regarding an important group, teacher leaders, their roles and responsibilities, and how their selection and development contribute to student learning. Whether your district or program is considering this position, actively utilizing these important members on your team, or contemplating improvements in this position, teachers and administrators will find this book informative, practical, and comprehensive." —**Dr. Barbara J. Phillips**, professor, Concordia University Chicago, former assistant superintendent for instruction, Skokie, IL District 68

"The authors provide an excellent basis for understanding both the informal and formal teacher leader. They provide a positive contribution for us as we learn the delicate dance of shared leadership." —**Julie Davis**, EdD, OAESA, executive director, Columbus, Ohio

"In this dynamically evolving period in educational leadership this comprehensive work clarifies the multifaceted role of the teacher leader. Outstanding work!" —**Colin Cameron**, director of programs, Confederation of Oregon School Administrators

"Tomal, Schilling, and Wilhite provide a comprehensive review of the latest and most effective educational leadership practices into one must-read text for teacher-leaders and administrators." —**Kadee Anstadt**, executive director of teaching & learning, Perrysburg Schools, Ohio

"*The Teacher Leader* addresses an essential role needed to improve the curriculum-instruction-assessment process through collaborative team work. This book nails this concept and identifies critical processes and skills to enhance this role in our schools today." —**Ron Warwick**, PhD, professor, Concordia University Chicago

"All educators and higher education faculty will find this book helpful in the development of a school culture that values collective inquiry and shared decision making." —**Dr. Lucy Ozvat**, ambassador and site coordinator for SAIL/CUC Partnership, Columbus, Ohio

"Teacher leadership expands the role of the leader to not only be positional power but to more realistically getting the job done. This book not only address the "why" but the "how" to make teacher leadership a reality. Since the future of school improvement and change rests with leadership, this is a concept and book that can't be missed." —**Margaret Trybus**, EdD, associate dean, College of Graduate and Innovative Programs, Concordia University Chicago

OTHER BOOKS BY THE AUTHORS

Action Research for Educators
Action Research for Educators, Second Edition
Challenging Students to Learn: How to Use Effective Leadership and Motivation Tactics
Discipline by Negotiation: Methods for Managing Student Behavior
How to Finish and Defend Your Dissertation: Strategies to Complete the Professional Practice Doctorate
Leading School Change: Maximizing Resources for School Improvement
Managing Human Resources and Collective Bargaining
Resource Management for School Administrators: Optimizing Fiscal, Facility, and Human Resources

The Teacher Leader

The Concordia University Chicago Leadership Series

An Educational Series from Rowman Littlefield Education

Education leaders have many titles and positions in American schools today: professors, K–12 teachers, district and building administrators, teacher coaches, teacher evaluators, directors, coordinators, staff specialists, etc. More than ever, educators need practical and proven educational and leadership resources to stay current and advance the learning of students.

Concordia University Chicago Leadership Series is a unique resource that addresses this need. The authors of this series are award-winning authors and scholars who are both passionate theorists and practitioners of this valuable collection of works. They give realistic and real-life examples and strategies to help all educators inspire and make a difference in school improvement and student learning that get results.

This Leadership Series consists of a variety of distinctive books on subjects of school change, research, completing advanced degrees, school administration, leadership and motivation, business finance and resources, human resource management, challenging students to learn, action research for practitioners, the teacher as a coach, school law and policies, ethics, and many other topics that are critical to modern educators in meeting the emerging and diverse students of today. These books also align with current federal, state, and various association accreditation standards and elements.

Staying current and building the future require the knowledge and strategies presented in these books. The Leadership Series originator, Daniel R. Tomal, Ph.D. is an award-winning author who has published over fifteen books and one hundred articles and studies, is a highly sought-after speaker and educational researcher. He along with his coauthors provide a wealth of educational experience, proven strategies that can help all educators aspire to be the best they can be in meeting the demands of modern educational leadership.

The Teacher Leader

Core Competencies and Strategies for Effective Leadership

Daniel R. Tomal, Craig A. Schilling, and Robert K. Wilhite

ROWMAN & LITTLEFIELD PUBLISHERS, INC.
Lanham • Boulder • New York • London

Published by Rowman & Littlefield
A wholly owned subsidiary of The Rowman & Littlefield Publishing Group, Inc.
4501 Forbes Boulevard, Suite 200, Lanham, Maryland 20706
www.rowman.com

16 Carlisle Street, London W1D 3 BT, United Kingdom

British Cataloging in Publication Information Available

Library of Congress Cataloging-in-Publication Data Available

978-1-4758-0744-8 (cloth : alk. paper)

∞™ The paper used in this publication meets the minimum requirements of American National Standard for Information Sciences—Permanence of Paper for Printed Library Materials, ANSI/NISO Z39.48-1992.

Printed in the United States of America.

In appreciation to all the teacher coaches, chairs, coordinators, and team leaders who act in the capacity of teacher leaders and the graduate teacher leader students at Concordia University Chicago.

Contents

Foreword

The Teacher Leader: Core Competencies and Strategies for Effective Leadership is a timely publication. Teacher leaders have always been present in schools but are now receiving the acknowledgment and attention they deserve. Any principal will accede that teacher leaders are indispensable members of school leadership teams whose work involves myriad activities covering every aspect of school life—both overt and behind-the-scenes pursuits—all of which are essential to the operations of an effective school.

Teacher leaders are involved in the complex intricacies of curriculum, assessment, and pedagogy. They are also involved in many other areas that may not be so obvious, including the recruitment, deployment, supervision, and professional learning of their colleagues; support for peer reflection and performance appraisal; being a "sounding board" for new ideas; and offering leadership for teams and networks within and outside schools. Teacher leaders also enable educational leaders such as principals and assistant principals to focus on whole school issues including, but going above and beyond, teaching and learning.

Teacher leadership is primarily about change and dealing with demands from multiple stakeholders—colleagues, students, parents, employers, education authorities, and numerous community groups—all of whom have differing expectations and requirements. Teacher leaders traverse the macro policy directives of federal and state governments, the policy demands of district education authorities, and must understand and successfully navigate the micro-politics of the school. They are change agents, coaches and mentors, motivators and resource managers. Teacher leaders are accountable and must abide by mandated standards, possess highly effective communication skills, build teams and a positive school culture, resolve conflicts, while retaining up-to-date knowledge about pertinent laws, policies, reforms, and issues affecting teaching and learning.

The greatest beneficiaries of teacher leaders are students. Teacher leaders provide the most direct means by which schools can improve pedagogical and assessment practices, raise student learning experiences and achievements, and ensure students' welfare and well-being. The diversity of students in our schools has never been greater and their learning needs are equally varied. Concurrently pressure is being placed on teachers to individualize programming and instruction to suit each individual's learning needs. This is a tall order and provides an insight to the complexity and importance of teacher leaders' work.

This book is highly practical, providing advice and ideas for those in the field and comes from a thorough understanding of the intensely political and diplomatic nature of teacher leaders' work. It provides contemporary research findings on the full range of applicable topics, case studies and sage advice, and an abundance of references and sources for further information. The book offers clear objectives, summaries, and reflective questions in each chapter.

The authors have a reputed history in research and publication in the area of educational leadership in its broadest sense. This latest edition adds to a stable of valuable resources for those involved in, aspiring to, or researching school leadership. This book emanates from long experience and extensive study and will be indispensable for teacher leaders or those aiming to hold such an exciting, important and professionally rewarding role in schools. I commend it to you.

Karen Starr, Ph.D.
FAICD FACEL FACE FIEDRC
Chair School Development and Leadership
Deakin University
Melbourne Burwood Campus, Australia

Acknowledgments

Appreciation is given to the many people who have assisted and worked with the authors. Special appreciation is given to the authors' students, colleagues, and associates who devote their lives and talents to educational leadership. The authors thank Susan Webb for her help in preparing the manuscript, and Laurel Schilling for her editorial review and suggestions.

The authors would also like to recognize and extend appreciation to the many teachers who serve as models of effective teaching and leadership. They are the real heroes in education. They make the difference for every child in a classroom. The authors would like to extend gratitude to the many people who endorsed this book and provided insight for this project. Lastly, the authors would like to thank their families for their support and unconditional love throughout this project.

Introduction

The teacher leader position is one that is becoming increasingly important and more frequent in K–12 public schools in the United States. This book has been written based upon years of study, research, and consulting in school leadership and administration. The models and strategies described in this book have been found successful in operating at multiple levels: department, unit, school building, and district.

Unlike other publications on school leadership, this book is specifically written for teacher leaders—coaches, chairs, coordinators, directors, etc.—and can be a valuable resource for practicing teacher leaders or students in university teacher leader programs. It can also be a good resource for all educators, especially students and teachers who aspire to become teacher leaders.

This book includes leadership topics that are essential in developing the knowledge and skills needed for educators to be successful school leaders. Topics are also selected to support leadership that promotes student learning and achievement. While primarily directed toward public schools, the strategies in this book can be effective for private elementary and secondary schools and charter schools. The principles and strategies are practical and useful for any school educator or graduate student who desires to improve his or her leadership skills and improve student learning.

Chapter 1 begins by addressing informal and formal teacher leaders. A brief history of the teacher leader movement is provided with emphasis placed on the teacher leader role in school improvement, climate, and culture. The *Teacher Leader Model Standards* are introduced and a link made with the *Intrastate School Leaders Licensure Consortium* (ISLLC) standards. Several examples of recent state initiatives in teacher leader endorsement programs are shared. The chapter ends with a case study on the role of a teacher leader in conducting a needs assessment for a school. Additional exercises and discussion questions are provided with a list of relevant references.

The next chapter establishes a review of the literature concerning the competencies, roles, functions, and dispositions of a teacher leader. Research is cited that illustrates these concepts leading directly to the *Teacher Leader Model Standards*. A study conducted by the authors is presented, which identifies ten core competencies of effective teacher leaders. A case study is included, which centers on using the *Teacher Leader Model Standards* as a guide in writing a job description. Additional exercises and questions are provided to expand knowledge in coaching and mentoring.

The third chapter provides practical examples in the application of the *Teacher Leader Model Standards* benchmarked with the ISLLC standards. The seven domains of the *Teacher Leader Model Standards* are explored and placed into a practical school context. Lastly, a comprehensive case study is provided for the teacher leader who may be applying for a position in a school. Additional exercises, questions, and references are provided.

Chapter 4 covers the topics of selecting, coaching, and mentoring. Several federal and state laws and guidelines are presented to help the teacher leader apply them to the responsibilities and functions of the teacher leader. Principles and strategies of interviewing and orientating new employees are covered. In addition several models and strategies are provided for coaching and mentoring employees as well as maintaining legal compliance. Lastly, a comprehensive case study along with exercises and discussion questions are provided to give the reader practice in applying the content of this chapter.

The next chapter covers the topic of leading and motivating a team. Several tried and proven theories and principles are given on leadership and motivation that can be applied directly to the teacher leader position. Also, the subject of building teamwork and accountability is presented along with several strategies and techniques. The chapter ends with a case study and exercises and discussion questions on leading and motivating employees.

The sixth chapter focuses on communicating, collaborating, and evaluating. Several models and strategies on managing conflict, active listening techniques, and communication styles are provided. Several strategies of teacher leader supervision such as conducting performance evaluations and setting goals with team members are given. The chapter concludes with a case study where the reader can test his or her ability in handling a typical teacher leader case situation.

Chapter 7 covers the role of the teacher leader in effecting change for instructional improvement. First is a discussion of why change is important to educators and teacher leaders. This is followed by a discussion of the teacher leader as a change agent including the types of change, leadership, and pedagogical skills required. Finally, the chapter concludes with a discussion of the challenges facing teacher leaders in the future.

Managing resources to promote student learning is the subject of the eighth chapter. After a discussion of the relationship between resources and student achievement, the chapter focuses on allocating resources to improve student performance. *Student-centric budgeting* is discussed in depth focusing on aligning resources with student learning and teacher needs. Finally, the chapter concludes with a discussion on managing technology resources.

The final chapter discusses the role of the teacher leader in the school improvement process. Several examples are provided, which demonstrate the various roles of teacher leaders. The focus is on *second-order change* at the school level and the difference a teacher leader can make in implementing school-wide change.

FEATURES OF THE BOOK

This book is succinctly written and an easy read for graduate students and practicing teacher leaders. This book is unique in that it provides many engaging examples that can be used by all teacher leaders. One feature of the book is the correlation of the each chapter's objectives with professional organizational standards of the *National Council for Accreditation of Teacher Education* (NCATE), the specialized professional association (SPA) of the *Educational Leadership Constituent Council* (ELCC), the *Interstate School Leaders Licensure Consortium* (ISLLC), National Education Association (NEA), and *Teacher Leader Model Standards* by *The Teacher Leadership Exploratory Consortium.*

Another valuable feature of the book is the incorporation of many teacher leadership strategies, processes, research, school improvement models, resources, and evaluation techniques. The information is presented in a straightforward and practical manner. The topics in this book are useful for any teacher leader or educator who desires to learn principles and strategies for coaching and leading teachers and staff.

Other features of this book include the following:

- practical examples of teacher leadership
- group motivation and collaboration
- strategies for leading and managing teams
- models of school-wide change and small-scale and group change

- a comprehensive description of resources needed for school improvement
- practical strategies in helping and teacher leaders understand and implement change
- examples of interviewing and conducting employee evaluations
- review of federal laws and guidelines for legal compliance as a teacher leader

Lastly, this book also contains a rich source of educational and reference websites for teacher leaders and all educators. The resources are the most up-to-date information on teacher leadership and reflect much of the various state standards on teacher leaders in public schools. This material should provide the essential foundation needed to be an effective teacher leader.

Chapter 1

Defining the
Teacher as Leader

OBJECTIVES

At the conclusion of this chapter, you will be able to:

1. Gain an understanding of the historical perspective of teacher leadership (ISLLC 6; ELCC 6; TLEC 2, 6; InTASC 4, 5, 6)
2. Understand why teacher leaders are needed in schools (ISLLC, 6; ELCC 6; TLEC 2, 6; InTASC 4, 5, 6)
3. Understand the impact of teacher leaders on school improvement (ISLLC 2, 3: ELCC 2, 3; TLEC 2, 4, 5; InTASC 1, 2, 3, 4, 5, 6, 7, 8, 9)
4. Review the link between the *Teacher Leader Model Standards* and the *Interstate School Leaders Licensure Consortium* (ISLLC) *Standards* (ISLLC 6; ELCC 6; TLEC 2, 7; InTASC 1, 4, 5, 6, 9, 10)
5. Review several state initiatives for teacher leadership (ISLLC 6; ELCC 6; TLEC 2, 7; InTASC 1, 4, 5, 6, 9, 10)

INFORMAL AND FORMAL TEACHER LEADERS

There have always been leaders in the teaching ranks of our schools. They are called by different names depending on their status or responsibilities within the faculty (see figure 1.1). There are teachers who have been in the school for decades having taught a multitude of families. They often teach the children of former students. These teachers are usually the most senior in the faculty of that school.

1

Their status as leader was gained through years of service provided to the school, knowledge of the community, and expert instructional pedagogy. They are often called the *revered teacher leaders*. Parents seek them out because these teachers are well known for quality of instruction and emotional links to families. Colleagues seek them out for advice, guidance, and support.

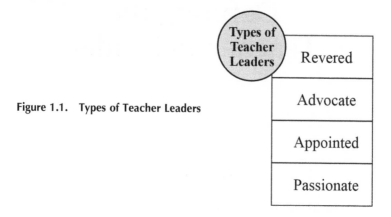

Figure 1.1.   Types of Teacher Leaders

There are those teachers who have earned the status of leader by virtue of their personality and collegiality. These *advocate teacher leaders* usually are the most vocal or most articulate about what matters most to the teachers in that school. Colleagues also seek them out for advice, guidance, and support. They are particularly important in a school where there is an active and strong union presence.

These *advocate teacher leaders* may serve a necessary role in helping to shape a professional climate that promotes teachers and students. They usually have the support of a majority of the faculty when it comes to working conditions and also have a voice in the school culture by virtue of their acceptance by their colleagues. They speak up when it comes to instructional materials, budget issues, school goals, and compensation issues.

There are *appointed teacher leaders* who are full or part-time in their positions and are responsible to guide and coordinate various programs within the school setting. They lead teams of teachers in initiatives that improve instruction, classroom practices, and the learning environment for children. These teacher leaders have many titles such as chairs, coordinators, supervisors, team leaders, or coaches. Some of these types of appointed teacher leaders even evaluate and supervise fellow teachers.

There are those teachers who are *passionate advocates* for children and usually speak up at every opportunity to help lead colleagues in developing student-centered curriculum. They promote programs that increase student engagement and work tirelessly to assist colleagues in improvement of classroom practices. They usually volunteer for curriculum committees, task forces, or small study groups to write and implement instructional programs that help to improve the performance of students in their schools.

While their titles may vary, there are some common traits informal and formal teacher leaders share as seen in figure 1.2. These traits may include altruism in working for the common good of all children. They are committed to children, colleagues, parents, and the communities they serve. They are passionate about their profession and motivated by what is the best interest of the students they serve.

Teacher leaders are collaborative and supportive, using shared leadership to build the capacity of their school, their team, and their colleagues. They are problem solvers who are motivated to solve challenges in seeking the best practices for increasing student performance.

The core of their work is to build teacher capacity, accountability, and teamwork.

Common Traits of Teacher Leaders

- Altruistic
- Collaborative
- Committed
- Motivated
- Passionate
- Problem Solver
- Student Centered
- Supportive

Figure 1.2. Common Traits of Teacher Leaders

Regardless of which type of teacher leader is examined, or any combination thereof, leaders in the teaching ranks have always had an active role in schools. The role can be defined by assumed duties, responsibilities, advocacy, or the status of having achieved a certain level of expertise in teaching pedagogy or content areas. These teachers provide valuable formal and informal insights, support, expertise, and professional development to their colleagues regardless of whether or not they receive compensation.

THE NEED FOR TEACHER LEADERS

In the past decade, there has been a movement to cultivate what the research and field call a teacher leader, which some state boards of education are formally endorsing on a professional teaching license. The role came about as a result of a combination of the accountability movement and a desire to improve schools. Such an example is seen in Illinois where the legislature passed a law entitled the Performance Evaluation Reform Act (PERA; Senate Bill 315; Public Act 96-0861).

This act mandated changes in the training and evaluation of teachers and principals by school and district leaders. Ancillary to this reform act there were changes to licensing of educators in Illinois. Illinois changed from a state where educators received various types of certificates to endorsements on licenses. Also a new teacher leader pathway was created to enhance and expand the knowledge and capacity of leaders for school changes.

Ohio recently created a teacher leader endorsement as well. After teachers earn a master's degree, they may take additional training in areas such as instruction, coaching and mentoring, assessment, and leadership strategies. Then, they may apply for the teacher leader endorsement on the teaching license.

Such changes like those in Illinois and Ohio have increased expectations for school leaders and training programs. State legislatures also have added increased stipulations for the funding schools receive based on student performance standards and school ratings. This has heightened interest in what schools do and how well it is done. As a consequence, lawmakers and parents have made educational improvement their shared mission.

In 2008, a group of educators formed the Teacher Leadership Exploratory Consortium for the purpose of examining current research about the leadership roles of teachers in student and school performance. These educators based their ideas on the premise that effective and collaborative teaching pedagogy leads to increased student achievement and improved decision making in schools.

In the Consortium publication, *Teacher Leader Model Standards*, is the stated reason why such standards exist. "The purpose of these standards—like all model standards—is to stimulate dialogue among stakeholders of the teaching profession about what constitutes the knowledge, skills, and competencies that teachers need to assume in leadership roles in their schools, districts, and the profession (*Teacher Leader Model Standards*, 2010, preface, page 3).

Consortium members asked themselves many questions about the roles and responsibilities teachers have in the school setting. Among these questions were the following:

1. Does one have to be a great teacher in order to be a teacher leader?
2. Is every teacher a teacher leader?
3. Can every teacher be a teacher leader?
4. What kinds of knowledge and skills must a teacher learn or develop to serve effectively as a teacher leader?
5. How should teacher leaders be selected?
6. How do we support teachers in leadership roles?

The Consortium panel developed seven *Teacher Leader Model Standards* (domains; see table 1.1.) of teacher leadership based on research and analysis of the current thinking in the field about teacher leaders. They envisioned that the domains would be used to help educators develop critical skills needed to

- research ideas.
- communicate best practices.
- collaborate among colleagues.

The standards (domains) describe the various aspects and *functions* of teacher leadership. These functions focus on teacher leader roles, dispositions, and activities that impact the day-to-day operations of the school. But more importantly, they focus on the learning climate and culture for student learning. These are critical aspects that are shown to increase student performance. These standards of teacher leaders are explored in later chapters.

Table 1.1. Teacher Leader Model Standards (Domains), 2010

Domain I	Fostering a collaborative culture to support educator development and student learning.
Domain II	Accessing and using research to improve practice and student learning.
Domain III	Promoting professional learning for continuous improvement.
Domain IV	Facilitating improvements in instruction and student learning.
Domain V	Promoting the use of assessments and data for school and district improvement.
Domain VI	Improving outreach and collaboration with families and community.
Domain VII	Advocating for student learning and the profession.

Source: Teacher Leader Exploratory Consortium

The *Teacher Leader Model Standards* are used to ensure that individuals who lead have acquired the knowledge, skills, and dispositions required to work with children and colleagues in a collaborative environment. These Consortium standards are specifically written for the teacher leader movement. However, there is another set of standards written for leadership effectiveness that is used to determine if individuals possess the knowledge and skills needed for schools today.

These ISLLC standards come from the work of the Council of Chief State School Officers (CCSSO). The CCSSO is a national organization of public officials who lead departments of education in the fifty states, the District of Columbia, the U.S. Department of Defense Education Division, and five United States territories.

ISLLC, 2011 (table 1.2) comprises of six standards that focus on knowledge, performance, and general disposition of leaders. These standards connect leader behavior to effective practices in the school setting. The standards have been developed through collaboration of many educators and input from several organizations.

The ISLLC standards address six broad areas of leadership. These standards will be presented with the *Teacher Leader Model Standards* in chapter three. The *Teacher Leader Model Standards* bridge the ISLLC standards in

Table 1.2. ISLLC Leadership Standards, 2011

Standard 1	Promotes the success of every student by facilitating the development, articulation, implementation, and stewardship of a vision of learning that is shared and supported by all.
Standard 2	Promotes the success of every student by advocating, nurturing, and sustaining a school culture and instructional program conducive to student learning and staff professional growth.
Standard 3	Promotes the success of every student by ensuring management of the organization, operation, and resources for a safe, efficient, and effective learning environment.
Standard 4	Promotes the success of every student by collaborating with faculty and community members, responding to diverse community interests and needs, and mobilizing community.
Standard 5	Promotes the success of every student by acting with integrity, fairness, and in an ethical manner.
Standard 6	Promotes the success of very student by understanding, responding to, and influencing the political, social, economic, legal, and culture context.

Source: Interstate School Leaders Licensure Consortium of Chief State School Officers, 2011

each of the six areas. In exploring the role of a teacher leader, the primary purpose of examining the two sets of standards is to establish a benchmark of those leadership traits, characteristics, and behaviors that will impact the day-to-day delivery and operations in schools.

In their vision of the teacher leader for the twenty-first century, the Consortium members identified five primary *focus areas* for teacher leadership (page 12, *Teacher Leader Model Standards*). They are as follows:

1. A teacher leader differs from other school leadership roles.
2. A teacher leader can enhance the capacity of the principal.
3. A teacher leader can support the strategies and behaviors linked to increasing student achievement.
4. A teacher leader will require a shift in the culture of the school.
5. A teacher leader requires new organizational structures and roles in schools in order to meet the needs and demands of the twenty-first-century learner.

The teacher leader should model effective practices, be capable of exercising their influence in various settings, and support collaborative collegial structures in their schools.

Central to the work of school reform is the pivotal role of school leadership (Murphy et al., 2006; Wagner et al., 2006). Traditionally, the principal has provided leadership, direction, and management of the school. Historically, such oversight included components of school administration, such as budgets, transportation, community involvement, discipline, and resource allocation (Reinhartz and Beach, 2004).

In addition to effective school management and administration, outcome-based and standards-based reform has made improvement of student learning the essential work of the leader of a school (Elmore, 2007). No longer can a school leader be successful if the knowledge base and skill set are not linked to instructional strategies. The central focus must be placed on effective teaching and student performance.

However, it is increasingly important for collective or shared leadership to be the model in today's schools. With the increasing demand on accountability and the focus on student achievement, it takes the collective wisdom of the entire faculty to make an effective school. Teacher leaders support the work of principals by creating a system of shared leadership allowing principals to delegate instructional leadership tasks to teacher leaders to alleviate their stress and to focus on high priority items.

Usually the teacher leader is a coach, a mentor, or a colleague who is there to support and guide a fellow teacher. Recently there has been movement in having teacher leaders also evaluate faculty in formal teacher evaluation programs. In states like Illinois, this formal aspect is added to the teacher leader endorsement in the public schools. This is done to add capacity for the principal who is often the only approved evaluator in a school setting.

Therefore two pathways emerge from the teacher leader movement. Pathway one is the coach or mentor who acts in a collegial capacity, and pathway two is a more formal teacher evaluator who acts in a supervisory capacity. With increasing accountability placed on school leaders, roles like these for teacher leaders add support for the important function of instructional improvement. More about these functions will be explored in later chapters.

Teacher leaders in schools also create more professional development providers in the building during a time when districts are being required to reduce administrative support. In teacher leaders, principals can recognize the expertise of teachers in subject matter knowledge, instructional practices, child development, and teacher needs. Using this knowledge, teacher leaders can perform various roles and responsibilities leading important tasks to enhance the quality of programs and improve teaching in the classrooms (see figure 1.3).

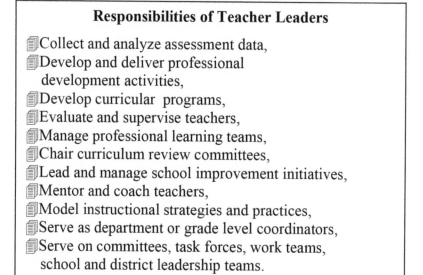

Responsibilities of Teacher Leaders

- Collect and analyze assessment data,
- Develop and deliver professional development activities,
- Develop curricular programs,
- Evaluate and supervise teachers,
- Manage professional learning teams,
- Chair curriculum review committees,
- Lead and manage school improvement initiatives,
- Mentor and coach teachers,
- Model instructional strategies and practices,
- Serve as department or grade level coordinators,
- Serve on committees, task forces, work teams, school and district leadership teams.

Figure 1.3.   **Responsibilities of Teacher Leaders**

Effective school leaders may use teacher leaders in a variety of roles. Sometimes they are called coaches (as in math or reading coaches), grade-level coordinators, directors, supervisors, or evaluators. Whatever terminology is used, the teacher leader role supports school improvement and increased student performance. Figure 1.4 lists various examples of teacher leader titles and roles.

Figure 1.4.   **Teacher Leader Roles and Titles**

SHARED LEADERSHIP AND SCHOOL IMPROVEMENT

Over the past several decades, preparation programs have been criticized for what many believe to be antiquated and ineffective methods of preparation and development (Marzano et al., 2005; Witziers et al., 2003). This well-documented need for change has prompted many states to evaluate their requirements for preparing school principals. Research also indicates that principals do not possess expertise in all of the best practices of curriculum, instruction, and assessment necessary to attain the academic goals for which they are being held accountable (Bottoms, 2001).

Without integral involvement of the teachers who possess diverse and specialized skills, school improvement efforts cannot achieve systematic progress toward sustainable goals. Principals need to recognize that the complex task of directing school improvement processes requires shared expertise. The collaboration of those who deliver instruction becomes central to the mission of improved instructional practice (Danielson, 2007; Elmore, 2007).

Consequently, collaborative leadership skills, which incorporate teacher expertise and decision making in policy and practice, are essential foundations of twenty-first-century school reform. Teacher leaders must be integral to this shared process of decision making. They can advance the skills of colleagues and form peer review teams to tackle the challenges of the school improvement processes.

A most recent addition to the knowledge base about shared leadership and collaboration has focused on *professional learning communities* (PLCs; DuFour et al., 2006; DuFour, 2008). State and federal accountability requirements place the burden of school success squarely on the shoulders of the school leadership and staff. Individual student achievement clearly must be the primary focus of the building principal and teachers. As a result, the principal's job description has expanded to that of *"chief child learning officer"* (Bottoms and O'Neill, 2001).

Principals need to know what students are supposed to learn and the standards they are to meet. They must have a working knowledge of research-based and student-centered instruction. They need to identify teachers who are exemplary in their practice and to support those who need more development in their methodology (Bottoms, 2001).

If schools are to be revitalized and improved, then school leaders must prepare for roles that facilitate mentoring and coaching and the development of positive school cultures (Murphy et al., 2006). The teacher leader can be a critical link to developing and supporting that culture of change and high expectations. Teacher leader functions and responsibilities as outlined in the *Teacher Leader Model Standards* clearly support this link.

Successful principals are those who balance leadership opportunities by making the best use of the people working around them. Based on effective leadership skills for school improvement, principals can use teacher leaders to expand diversity in leadership styles and practice. They can collaborate with teacher leaders who guide their colleagues on the design and delivery of instruction. Teacher leaders can be used to identify problems of teacher practice and study solutions to expand the expertise of colleagues.

A key role where principals can use teacher leaders is in recruitment and hiring of teachers. However, their most valuable role can be in mentoring, coaching, and evaluating the professional practices of faculty. Teacher leaders can conduct and evaluate professional development activities geared to the instructional growth of colleagues. They can be used effectively to assist colleagues in the evaluation of student work. They can be key players in the development of strategic plans that promote diversity and allocation of equitable resources to promote student growth.

According to Murphy et al. (2006), a comprehensive overview of the requisite skills for school leadership encompasses a number of dimensions. These include vision for learning, instructional and curricular programming, assessment procedures, and data analysis for improved student learning, communities of professional practice, allocation and use of resources, positive organizational cultures, and social advocacy. Principals can delegate some of these dimensions to teacher leaders. Teacher leader instructional expertise can be used effectively in instructional and curricular programming, assessment and data analysis, and managing professional communities.

Amidst these possible changes, school leaders also face cultural resistance to changing their roles and reforming their schools due to past practice. The reasons for the resistance are many. Schools and teachers still operate in a high degree of isolation (silos), which make a culture of collaboration difficult. Past leader roles are steeped in hierarchical structures of positional authority, which have been deeply engrained in school communities' conception of a leader.

Increased test-based accountability demands put pressure on leaders to attend to short-term management solutions rather than long-term, collaborative growth solutions (Braun, Gable, and Kite, 2008). Such barriers to change must be overcome by school leaders before meaningful school improvement can be achieved. Effective use of the teacher leader to assist in these reform efforts can improve the climate for change and help teachers to overcome their personal feelings and perceived or engrained institutional barriers.

DuFour (2008), highlighting the importance of collaborative leadership skills, comments, "They (school leaders) recognize and value the collective wisdom residing within the school, and they create the structures and culture to allow staff members to tap into that wisdom. They are religiously attentive to establishing positive relationships with and among teachers" (p. 3). The teacher leader must possess these same dimensions of leadership.

Similarly, Danielson (2007) states, "To be successful in these roles, teacher leaders need to develop expertise in curriculum planning, assessment design, data analysis . . . the ability to listen actively, facilitate meetings, keep a group discussion on track, decide on a course of action, and monitor progress" (p. 17). The process of collaborative learning provides a mechanism to increase individual teacher capacity. By putting issues of teaching and learning at the center of the dialogue, it becomes the primary focus among the entire school community.

Further, through the cooperative work of principals and teachers focusing on continuous student and faculty learning, research has shown an increase in student performance. The school principal needs to have expertise in instruction, the ability to use data as evidence to support decisions, and the ability to leverage resources that yield the best results for students. These are areas where teacher leaders can provide support services and resources to enhance the school community and the expertise of the teaching staff.

DuFour et al. (2006) refer to this as a shift from a focus on *teaching* to a focus on *learning*. When a teacher comments that it is not his or her job to make sure all the kids in class learn, this is evidence that the teacher does not understand the difference between teaching and learning. When a teacher leader coaches a colleague in understanding student performance outcomes versus classroom strategies, the teacher leader has made the shift in thinking and chances are so has that teacher.

Unfortunately, the tradition in American public education has been that only administrators push for changes that benefit students and that it is the job of teachers to hold out for what is convenient and comfortable for themselves and their colleagues. Teacher contract language in many districts has been crafted to guarantee certain working conditions for teachers. Too often this keeps the focus riveted on teaching and makes the shift to a focus on learning more difficult.

In schools that are working to become increasingly effective, PLCs are the framework most suited to putting research-based practices and policies in place. Teacher leaders are the ideal lynchpin of this work. They are the one who can help to change the focus on learning. A knowledgeable and effective teacher leader could lead the work of each grade level or course team to achieve this shift in thinking.

Administrators alone cannot lead these teams. In the first place, there are not enough administrators to lead them all, nor do administrators have the time to do so. Certainly they do not have the knowledge of individual students and the depth of curriculum expertise that the teachers have. The principal must lead and orchestrate the overall effort, assisted by the assistant principals in schools that have them, but teachers must lead their own teams.

In effective schools, a culture of professional inquiry and collaborative practice needs to flourish. The principal needs to be confident in and respected for content expertise and professional skill. The principal must develop interpersonal skills that command credibility among peers and colleagues. Using teacher leaders who are trained in data management and collaborative teaming practices, principals can set the overall tone for efforts toward continuous improvement of student learning.

Dispositions of flexibility and openness to change are essential if principals and teacher leaders are to guide the development of professional learning communities and the examination of current practices (DuFour et al., 2006; Wagner et al., 2006). By mobilizing the expertise and cooperation of faculty and faculty leaders, principals create pathways for significant student academic growth that have a dynamic impact on the school's culture. The link to culture in discussions of instructional leadership and school improvement validates the importance of school climate in student and teacher performance.

Culture includes the norms, shared beliefs, rituals, and assumptions of the organization. As reviewed in the literature, there are multiple perspectives of the skills and traits required for effective school leadership. However, nearly all of these perspectives support the importance of leaders who develop and maintain positive relationships with staff members. Positive relationships have a profound effect on school climate and culture. These perspectives will be discussed in future chapters.

Developing and maintaining positive relationships with staff is a critical component of nurturing a positive climate. When there are cultures that are more positive, teacher performance will be better and lead to improved student performance. School leaders will be wise to use teacher leaders who are known by the staff to have good rapport and positive relationships. These teacher leaders have proven credibility and can guide colleagues in the improvement of the day-to-day instruction in the classroom.

The ability to manage change processes is a vital component for the successful leadership of schools as well. The leadership skills needed for collaborative work involve the ability to develop a shared sense of purpose with colleagues. Using teacher leaders to facilitate group processes and communicate well gives an added dimension to this leadership process and adds capacity to the decision-making process of the school staff.

Effective school leaders make use of successful teacher leaders who understand collaboration and change and the effect on people while mediating conflict in the change process as seen in figure 1.5. Most importantly, they must understand that effective teacher leaders must hold a realistic understanding of adult learning.

Leadership Skills for the Change Process

- Develop leadership credibility,
- Communicate effectively,
- Develop a shared sense of purpose,
- Facilitate group processes,
- Practice adult learning strategies,
- Mediate conflict,
- Collaborate the change processes,
- Monitor and evaluate the outcomes.

Figure 1.5. Leadership Skills for the Change Process

A leader needs to be prepared in the real context of schools to confront resistance to change and develop the resilience to support it (Gabriel, 2005). With training in change theory and management, the teacher leader can embrace the responsibility of an active contributor to the school community. Acknowledging that addressing real change often involves risk and conflict, the teacher leader can work with the principal to effect systematic change and to actively advocate for the success of all students.

A cutting-edge study to first tackle questions of what works in a large-scale, systematic way was Mid-Continent Research for Education and Learning (McREL), which conducted a meta-analysis of decades of studies of teachers' classroom practice, selecting the most rigorous from an initial sampling of four thousand such studies. McREL's researchers mathematically determined the most effective practices found to have a statistically significant impact on student learning measured by standardized test scores.

First published in 2001, this study, described in *Classroom Instruction That Works* (Marzano et al., 2001), revolutionized teaching by linking classroom strategies to evidence of increased student learning. The basic premise of the study was to show that schools that use research to guide instructional practices outperform those that do not.

In a companion book, *What Works in Schools*, Marzano (2003) describes eleven research-based factors shown in another large-scale research project at McREL to be essential for the larger context of an effective school. These factors were categorized into three areas of school, teacher, and student factors.

The *school factors* were a guaranteed and viable curriculum, challenging goals and effective feedback, parent and community involvement, a safe and orderly environment, and collegiality and professionalism. The *teacher factors* were instructional strategies, classroom management, and effective curriculum design. The *student factors* were home environment, learned intelligence and background knowledge, and motivation. These eleven factors led to the conclusion that school effectiveness and teacher effectiveness are highly interrelated in how a student learns (Marzano, 2003).

In his 90-90-90 studies, Reeves (2005) showed that high-poverty schools could also be high performing. He provided examples from multiple school systems to illustrate the common characteristics of 90-90-90 schools (over 90 percent poverty, over 90 percent minorities, and yet over 90 percent achieving at high proficiency levels). The factors identified in the studies were a strong focus on academic achievement, clear curriculum choices, frequent assessment of student progress and multiple opportunities for improvement, an emphasis on nonfiction writing, and collaborative scoring of student work, with explicit guidelines.

He stressed that teacher quality and effective leadership, not demographics, are the most dominant factors in determining student success. The effective practices and policies identified in those studies are entirely consistent with the McREL's findings. It is these types of studies that effective leaders can use to improve the teaching and learning in schools.

Principals can use the teacher leader to guide the PLCs in analysis and application of such research as it impacts the day-to-day learning and instruction in the classroom. Many states have moved in the direction of research-based instructional decision making. Such policy direction has helped the influence of the teacher leader movement. In the next section, several state initiatives are examined to illustrate this focus on instructional practices and teacher professional development to improve student learning.

STATE INITIATIVES IN TEACHER LEADERSHIP

Research in teacher and principal leadership strongly suggests that effective teaching practices be based on sound data collection and analysis with direct linkage to student learning outcomes. Aligning this notion to the *Teacher Leader Model Standards* and ISLLC leadership policy standards, there is the inference that teachers in a collaborative shared leadership model using the standards as tools will better meet the accountability goals of higher expectations for learning and increased student performance.

State departments of education have embarked on these initiatives as a result of the help from the federal legislation, No Child Left Behind, and most recently the Race-to-the-Top monies allocated by the U.S. Department of Education. These federal initiatives have raised the issue of accountability and placed it squarely on the shoulders of state agencies, school districts, and universities and institutions of teacher preparation.

State legislators want more accountability and higher student performance. The teacher leader movement supports these needs and suggests effective skills, disposition, and competencies to supplement and support the leadership of schools. Many states have moved ahead with the *Teacher Leader Model Standards* to establish training programs for teacher leaders and create pathways for this purpose. The following sample programs outline just a few of the state initiatives in the past five years. It is certain that more will follow in the future.

In Illinois, the Illinois State Board of Education (ISBE) created a pathway for a teacher leader endorsement. This provides state recognition for teachers who serve in these roles and have acquired additional leadership training. The endorsement permits teachers who want to pursue additional leadership training and responsibilities but want to still remain a teacher to do so without having to complete a full administrative licensure program.

The teacher leader endorsement added to the Illinois professional educator license (PEL) can be acquired seeking a master's degree. Or, additional post–master's work can be done in course areas such as assessment, coaching, mentoring, adult learning, social and emotional needs of children, supervision training, and curriculum development.

In Ohio, the Ohio Board of Regents created a pathway for a teacher leader endorsement. This endorsement on the teaching license provides a state recognition for teachers who serve in these roles and have acquired additional leadership training. It also allows teachers who want to pursue additional leadership training and responsibilities but want to still remain a teacher to do so without having to complete a full administrative licensure program. The teacher leader endorsement is acquired only postmaster's in Ohio.

In Louisiana, all teacher leader programs are performance based, and aspiring teacher leaders must meet all ISLLC/ELCC and Louisiana state leadership standards. Teachers must complete two graduate level courses in school leadership. These two courses articulate into a full educational leadership program.

The Louisiana program is aimed at teachers who do not want to become administrators but still want to be leaders in their schools. Typically, these leaders want to be grade level or department chairs. The endorsement has allowed teacher leaders to better understand the principal's role and the needs of the position. The endorsement does not mandate a pay raise. This is at the discretion of the district. There are no building-level positions that require teachers to have this endorsement.

Georgia has recently adopted a policy that created a state teacher leader endorsement. Teacher leader programs are performance based and must address two leadership standards for teacher leaders: 1) facilitate the development, articulation, implementation, and stewardship of a shared vision; and 2) promote a positive school culture, provide an effective instructional program, apply research best practices, and design comprehensive professional growth plans for staff. The teacher leader endorsement does not mandate a pay raise. The teacher leader program should provide a career pathway into full school leader certification.

In California, the San Juan Unified School District negotiated an article in the teacher's contract (Article 24—Creating and Sustaining a Collaborative Culture) with the teacher's union.

It establishes leadership teams in all district schools made up of faculty, principal, and a assistant principal. The charge of the leadership teams are to focus on continuous improvement of the teacher, student learning and quality instruction, broaden the leadership base, build a professional learning community, and model leadership to other community members.

The agreement stipulates that every Thursday is an early release day and teachers are required to stay and engage in a collaborative activity with their colleagues to improve student achievement. The school leadership team develops the agenda and activity. The leadership team is responsible for planning three annual staff development days. Leadership teams are elected by their peers and serve a three-year term. Members of leadership teams earn a stipend. The impact of the leadership teams has led teachers to become more intensively engaged in examining student data, determining gaps in performance, and developing action steps to address the gaps.

This is just a sample of what some states are doing to encourage teachers to move into school and district leadership roles. The overall purpose is to improve student learning. The ancillary outcomes include increased capacity for leadership in the schools, enhanced focus on assessment, increased professional development and training for teachers, and more direct linkage to school improvement goals.

SUMMARY

Teacher leaders are needed to promote and advance effective leadership in a school. Successful principals know how to utilize teacher leaders who process skills and traits that maximize learning and develop increased teacher instructional strategies. The *Teacher Leader Model Standards* and the ISLLC standards combine to form a framework for those competencies and leadership skills that identify an effective teacher leader. States are now rolling out preparation programs to provide pathways for training and licensure in teacher leadership.

CASE STUDY

Jefferson School District — Reading Needs Assessment

You have been selected and hired as a teacher leader. The first assignment given to you by your principal is to conduct a *needs assessment* of the reading program. Standardized test scores in reading indicate a drop in student performance. A needs assessment is the process for determining an organization's needs and gaps in relation to a desired outcome or list of wants/goals. The purpose of this particular assessment is to summarize the needs of your school and to recommend effective classroom strategies to improve reading instruction. The format of the needs assessment report is as follows.

1. Introduction
   What are characteristics of the school?

2. Problem statement
   What are the central issues in your schools concerning reading?
3. Current state of instructional practices
   Include relevant information from interviews with teachers.
4. Observed classroom strategies
   What are the strengths and weaknesses of the reading instruction observed?
5. Gaps and needs
   Define the major gaps and needs of the instructional strategies and materials.
6. Conclusion
   Include a brief summary conclusion and recommendations.

EXERCISES AND DISCUSSION QUESTIONS

1. How did the role of each teacher add to the effectiveness of the needs assessment?
2. What characteristics of shared leadership were needed for this needs assessment?
3. What role did the teacher leader play in shared leadership?
4. What obstacles were encountered in this needs assessment? What problem solving skills were needed?
5. Interview a school principal and ask why principals alone cannot manage schools of today.

REFERENCES

Bottoms, G. (2001). *What school principals need to know about curriculum and instruction.* Atlanta, GA: Southern Regional Education Board.

Bottoms, G. and O'Neill, K. (2001). *Preparing a new breed of school principals: It's time for action.* Atlanta, GA: Southern Region Education Board.

Braun, D., Gable, R., and Kite, S. (2008). *Relationship among essential leadership preparation practices and leader, school, and student outcomes in K-8 schools.* Paper presented at the annual meeting of the Northeastern Educational Research Association, Rocky Hill, CT.

Danielson, C. (2006). *Teacher leadership that strengthens professional practice.* Alexandria, VA: Association for Supervision and Curriculum Development.

Danielson, C. (2007). The many faces of leadership. *Educational Leadership, 65*(1), 14–19.

DuFour, R. (Ed.), (2008). *The collaborative administrator.* Bloomington, IN: Solution Tree.

DuFour, R., DuFour, R., Eaker, R., and Many, T. (2006). *Learning by doing: A handbook for professional learning communities at work*. Bloomington, IN: Solution Tree.

Educational Leadership Consortium Council, *ELCC Standards* (2002). Washington, DC, National Policy Board for Educational Administration (NPBEA).

Elmore, R. (2007). *School reform from the inside out: Policy, practice and performance*. Cambridge, MA: Harvard Education Press.

Futrell, M. H., and Kelly, J. A. (2001). *Leadership for student learning: Redefining the teacher as leader. School leadership for the 21st century initiative: A report of the taskforce on teacher leadership*. Washington, DC: Institute for Educational Leadership.

Gabriel, J. (2005). *How to thrive as a teacher leader*. Alexandria, VA: Association for Supervision and Curriculum Development.

Interstate School Leaders Licensure Consortium, *ISLLC standards* (2011). Washington DC, Interstate School Leaders Licensure Consortium of Chief State School Officers.

Marzano, R. (2003). *What works in schools: Translating research into action*. Alexandria, VA: Association for Supervision and Curriculum Development.

Marzano, R., Pickering, D., and Pollock, J. (2001). *Classroom instruction that works: Research based strategies for increasing student achievement*. Alexandria, VA: Association of Supervision and Curriculum Development.

Marzano, R., Waters, R., and McNulty, B. (2005). *School leadership that works: From research to result*. Alexandria, VA: Association of Supervision and Curriculum Development.

Murphy, J., Elliott, S., Goldring, E., and Porter, A. (2006). *Learning-centered leadership: A conceptual foundation*. A paper commissioned by The Wallace Foundation, New York.

Reeves, D. B., (2005). *Accountability in action: A blueprint for learning organizations* (2nd ed.). Denver, CO: Advanced Learning Press.

Reinhartz, J., and Beach, D. (2004). *Educational leadership: Changing schools, changing roles*. Boston, MA: Allyn and Bacon.

Teacher Leader Model Standards (2010). Teacher Leader Exploratory Consortium. Washington, DC. www.teacherleaderstandards.org/

Wagner, T., Kegan, R., Lahey, L., Lemons, R., Garnier, J., Helsing, D., Howell, A., and Rasmussen, H. T. (2006). *Change leadership: A practical guide to transforming our schools*. San Francisco, CA: Jossey-Bass.

Witziers, B., Bosker, R. J., and Kruger, M. L. (2003). Educational leadership and student achievement: The elusive search for an association. *Educational Administration Quarterly, 39*(3), 398–425.

Chapter 2

The Nature of
Teacher Leaders

OBJECTIVES

At the conclusion of this chapter, you will be able to:

1. Gain a perspective of teacher leadership capacities and practices (ISLLC 6; ELCC 6; TLEC 2, 6; InTASC 1, 2, 3, 4, 5, 6, 10)
2. Understand teacher leader roles and dispositions reviewed in the literature (ISLLC 6; ELCC 6; TLEC 2, 6; InTASC 1-10)
3. Understand ten key competencies for the teacher leader (ISLLC 2, 3; ELCC 2, 3; TLEC 2, 4, 5, InTASC 1-10)
4. Review the link between the literature and a research study investigating the ten core competencies (ISLLC 6; ELCC 6; TLEC 2, 7; InTASC 1, 9, 10)
5. Review ten teacher leader competencies in the context of leadership standards (ISLLC 6; ELCC 6; TLEC 2, 7; InTASC 1, 9, 10)

TEACHER LEADER PATHWAYS

In *The Many Faces of Leadership*, Charlotte Danielson (2007) called teaching *a flat profession*. She suggested that in most professions, the more knowledge and expertise one gains, the more responsibility one assumes; but, in teaching, "The 20-year veteran's responsibilities are essentially the same as those of the newly licensed novice" (p. 14).

Most teachers are aware of the many headaches and accountability issues that come with being a school leader. There are budgets, facilities, management, contracts, evaluations, community relations, and endless meetings. Usually, many teachers only want input into those instructional programming, materials, and practices that influence their day-to-day teaching and classrooms. The question then is how do teachers assume more responsibility for leadership in their schools?

A survey of the literature revealed that there were multiple research studies in the field of teacher leadership covering multidimensional topics. There were studies that included, but were not limited to, examinations of *effective leadership styles* such as those by Anderson (2004); Leithwood and Jantzi (2000); Lucas and Valentine (2002); Harris (2002); Spillane, Halverson, and Diamond (2001); Ross and Gray (2006); and Tickle, Brownlee, and Nailon (2005). There were studies that focused on *job satisfaction and motivation* such as those by Bye, Pushkar, and Conway (2007); Herzberg (2006); and Remedios and Boreham (2004).

There were studies that covered *descriptions and models for structure* such as those by Bauer, Haydel, and Cody (2003); Cuban (2008); and Hatch, White, and Faigenbaum (2005); and a study discovered on *how to promote teachers and the barriers involved in teacher leadership* by Beachum and Dentith (2004). All of these studies were focused on specific topics in teacher leadership. The studies added to the literature by identifying important characteristics and dispositions of teacher leaders.

However, research that focused on *skills* and *traits* seemed to best outline the pathway for the teacher leader to assume leadership roles in the school. These studies included *identity and efficacy* by Leithwood and Beatty (2008) and Nieto (2003). There were studies on *teacher leader perspectives* and *perceptions* by Barth (2001); Bowman (2004); Dozier (2007); Gonzales (2004); Katzenmeyer and Moller (2009); Lieberman and Walker (2007); and Rogers (2005).

Using teacher and administrator comments and their shared perceptions, these studies identified key skills, traits, and competencies that led to leadership roles for the teacher leader. These perspectives will be closely examined in this chapter as they relate to the *Teacher Leader Model Standards*.

We know that teacher leaders are both teachers and leaders. They exercise professional responsibilities both in and out of the classroom (Katzenmeyer and Moller, 2009). Much of the literature indicated teacher leaders often have significant teaching experience and demonstrate *expertise, collaboration, reflection,* and *a sense of empowerment*.

Teacher leaders seek challenges and growth, and they go out of their way to find innovative and challenging programs to increase the learning of their students and their colleagues. They enable others to act, are risk takers, and collaborators. Descriptions in the studies of these teachers included attributes of assuming desirable personal traits such as being *dependable, supportive,* and *informally reassuring to colleagues.*

It was common to find that among group members there were individuals who communicated better than others and seemed to have the unusual competence to overcome conflicts and solve problems (York-Barr and Duke, 2004). Such traits of conflict resolution and problem solving are explored later in this chapter. They are often cited in the literature as key skills of an effective teacher leader.

TEACHER LEADER ROLES AND FUNCTIONS

Teacher leadership involves varying roles or functions. But most of the functions involve teacher leaders engaged in *collaboration* and school *instructional decision-making* processes, as well as demonstrating and *sharing instructional expertise* with colleagues. As suggested in chapter one, this can be an informal or formal position with authority in which the teacher leader is reviewing and studying best classroom practices.

They can be engaging in dialog aimed at instructional or student improvement. They mentor, collaborate, model practices, or help to broaden other's understandings (Ackerman and Mackenzie, 2006). Teacher leadership serves as a logical model for teachers and administrators to support one another in transforming their practices in this current environment of ever-increasing accountability (Beachum and Dentith, 2004).

Other functions have been identified in the literature as well. Silva, Gimbert, and Nolan (2000) and Barth (2001) identified areas of essential teacher leader work as being textbook selection, curriculum, standards for student behavior, student tracking, staff development, promotion and retention policies, budgets, teacher evaluations, selecting new staff, selecting new administrators, budgets, and professional development.

Wetig's (2002) study of teacher leaders revealed that those who studied *facilitated change* were involved in *mentoring* and were teachers who exhibited *best practices in their instruction.* Wetig also suggested teacher leaders were instrumental when acting in roles as team leaders, department chairpersons, mentors, master teachers, grade level chairs, curriculum coordinators, or consultants. These teacher leader roles were mentioned consistently in the literature.

Dozier's (2007) survey of three hundred accomplished teacher leaders revealed their personal beliefs of contribution included their work of *building relationships* through professional development facilitators, working in curriculum development, serving as department chairs, grade chairs, and mentors to other teachers.

Such studies as Ackerman and Mackenzie (2006) and Silva, Gimbert, and Nolan (2000) of teacher leadership also identified department chairs, school improvement team leaders, and leaders of professional development for teachers as formal roles which are inexplicably associated with teacher leadership.

Another function often highlighted in the literature is the *influence teacher leaders exercise in their work*. Whether formal or informal positions were identified, most alluded to or directly named responsibilities supported by the idea of influencing others toward improved student performance through school improvement efforts (Barth, 2001; Crowther, Kaagan, Ferguson, and Hann, 2002).

Research by Harris and Muijs (2005) suggested that *collaboration* concerned with improved student learning is at the heart of teacher leadership. As mentioned earlier, research that focused on skills or traits came closest to the standards established by the Teacher Leader Consortium (see table 1.1). A key question arises, if teacher leadership provides a pathway for teachers to have direct connections to decisions and operations influencing the day-to-day instruction in their classrooms, then what are the most important competencies to achieve this pathway?

Another review of table 1.1 clearly illustrates the *Teacher Leader Model Standards* that Consortium members suggested are needed for successful teacher leadership. Research during the last two decades has emphasized that teacher leadership is integral to successful whole-school reform. The research also demonstrated that teacher effectiveness contributed more to improving student academic outcomes than any other school characteristic.

These same studies also suggested that an effective leader is central to recruiting and supporting teachers and leading school improvement (Murphy et al., 2006; Rivkin et al., 2005; Waters et al., 2003). A student who has great teachers for several consecutive years will be on a path of continued growth and success, while a student who was taught by a succession of less effective teachers may experience lasting academic challenges (Hanushek and Rivkin, 2009).

Jackson and Bruegmann (2009) suggested that teachers learn from other effective teachers in their schools and are more likely to raise student achievement when they are surrounded by colleagues who are effective at raising achievement.

Second only to classroom instruction, school leadership is the most important school-based variable affecting student achievement (Leithwood et al., 2004). The school leader affects student achievement in many ways, including playing a critical role in *creating a school culture focused on learning* and *high expectations* (Murphy et al., 2006).

The school leader also affects the quality of the instructional staff through hiring decisions and professional development activities (Papa et al., 2003). Teachers cite a principal's support and effectiveness as a leading factor that contributes to their decision to remain in teaching (Futernick, 2007).

It is from these ranks of teachers that teacher leaders are cultivated and developed. These teacher leaders support the higher expectations of a school's mission. They support and assist their colleagues in meeting important and critical goals to improving student learning.

A pattern emerges in the literature concerning leadership. Effective school leaders who build the capacity for shared leadership and collaboration in their schools make use of successful teacher leaders and other support staff to build a climate and culture of continuous school improvement focused on the primary goal of improved student performance.

SUCCESSFUL LEADERSHIP FACTORS

In an early study of school leaders by Wendell, Hoke, and Josekel (1993), several significant factors were identified that contributed to school leader success. These included *effective communications, collaborative leadership, risk taking, community outreach, positive staff relations,* and *having a clear personal philosophy.*

Another study by Elmore (2007) suggested successful leaders *collaborate* on the design and delivery of instruction; *identify* problems of practice and study solutions; *conduct and evaluate* professional development; *evaluate* student work; *recruit and hire* teachers; mentor, *coach,* and *evaluate* the professional practice of faculty; *develop* strategic plans that *promote* diversity and *allocate* equitable resources to promote student growth.

These same factors also mirror the *Model Teacher Leader* and ISLLC standards. Whether it is an administrator or a teacher leader, the successful leaders need skills to accomplish the vision, mission, and goals of the school. These indicators form the beginning core of skills necessary for successful leadership in a school with high expectations and high student learning.

According to Murphy et al. (2006), a comprehensive overview of the requisite skills for school leadership encompasses a number of dimensions. They include a vision for learning, instructional and curricular programming, assessment procedures and data analysis for improved student learning, communities of professional practice, allocation and use of resources, positive organizational cultures, and social advocacy.

These skills nearly mirror word for word the *Model Teacher Leader Standards* (table 1.1) and the ISLLC standards (table 1.2). Similarly, Danielson (2007) stated teacher leaders need to develop expertise in curriculum planning, assessment design, data analysis, and the ability to listen actively, facilitate meetings, keep a group discussion on track, decide on a course of action, and monitor progress.

The Center for Comprehensive School Reform and Improvement suggested in 2005 that the tasks performed by teacher leaders include *monitoring* improvement efforts, *selecting* curriculum, and *participating* in administrative meetings. In addition, they often are called upon to participate in *peer coaching, engage parent and community* participation, and *review research* in their time away from the classroom.

As the research studies revealed, the various traits of an effective teacher leader mirror those of a school leader. However, special emphasis is placed on the critical skills of instructional decision making and improved teaching strategies.

A set of common core competencies necessary for the effective teacher leader emerged from the review of the literature. The core competencies most often cited were mentoring and coaching teachers, leading and motivating staff, improving curriculum and instruction, managing resources, building collaboration, managing school change, communicating to staff, conducting teacher evaluations, and building community relations (see figure 2.1).

A STUDY OF TEACHER LEADER CORE COMPETENCIES

Based on these core competencies, Tomal and Wilhite investigated the concept of effective teacher leader practices as identified in the literature. The literature reviewed for the study included numerous small-scale studies that described dimensions of teacher leadership practice, teacher leader characteristics, and conditions that promote and challenge teacher leadership. The purpose of the study was to obtain the opinions of current public school teacher leaders to determine the most valued of the core competencies.

The basis of this study came from recent legislative initiatives in such states as Illinois and Ohio where *teacher leader endorsement programs* were developed to help prepare future teacher leaders in the core competencies most valued by experienced school administrators and professors. There were two questions for this study:

1. What are the most important core competencies for teacher leaders for public schools?
2. Is there a significant difference in the importance of the core competencies between teacher coaches and teacher leader evaluators?

The participants in this study consisted of forty K–12 public school *teacher leader evaluators* (those teacher leaders who supervise and conduct

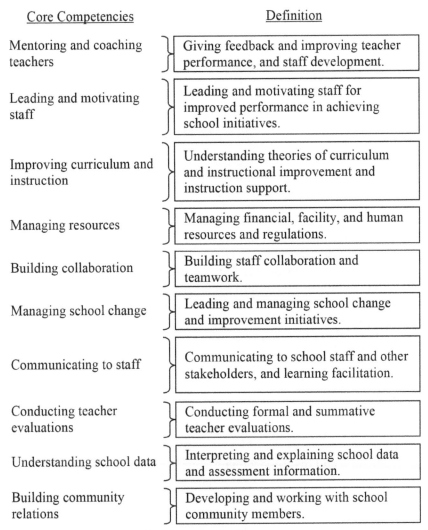

Core Competencies	Definition
Mentoring and coaching teachers	Giving feedback and improving teacher performance, and staff development.
Leading and motivating staff	Leading and motivating staff for improved performance in achieving school initiatives.
Improving curriculum and instruction	Understanding theories of curriculum and instructional improvement and instruction support.
Managing resources	Managing financial, facility, and human resources and regulations.
Building collaboration	Building staff collaboration and teamwork.
Managing school change	Leading and managing school change and improvement initiatives.
Communicating to staff	Communicating to school staff and other stakeholders, and learning facilitation.
Conducting teacher evaluations	Conducting formal and summative teacher evaluations.
Understanding school data	Interpreting and explaining school data and assessment information.
Building community relations	Developing and working with school community members.

Figure 2.1. Core Competencies of Teacher Leaders

teacher evaluations) and thirty-three K–12 public school *teacher leader coaches* in selected elementary and secondary schools in northeast Illinois.

The participants largely consisted of Chicago public schools and Chicago suburban school district teachers. Teacher leaders were defined as any teacher working in the capacity of a team leader, department chair, coordinator, or lead teacher role. They came from diverse economic, cultural, ethnic, gender, and academic backgrounds.

A two-part questionnaire was used in this study. Part one consisted of a list of the ten core competencies in which the respondents were asked to rate the competencies based upon their importance for performing the job of a teacher leader (see figure 2.1).

The second part consisted of an open-ended question that asked the respondents to describe any other core competencies that were important for a teacher leader serving in this type of capacity in public schools. Space was given for other comments the respondents wanted to add. In some cases, follow-up interviews were conducted with the respondents to gain further information concerning the core competencies and responsibilities of the positions.

The survey instrument consisted of ten core competencies developed by Tomal and Wilhite (2014) based upon the Illinois and Ohio teacher leader endorsement standards, *The Model Teacher Leader Standards*, and related research. The core competencies were validated through a series of expert reviews.

Definitions were created to assist the respondents in defining each of the core competencies (see figure 2.1). A series of interviews were conducted with teacher leaders in helping to determine the core competencies and definitions. A standard Likert scale (5 = most important and 1 = least important) was used. Also, the scale included the option of 0 indicating that the teacher leaders found the core competency to be irrelevant given they did not have job responsibilities in that area.

The survey included identification of two types of teacher leaders. Respondents were asked to identify themselves as either a *teacher leader coach* (having no responsibility for formally evaluating teachers) or a *teacher leader evaluator* (having responsibility for formally evaluating teachers). All the respondents were acting in a full-time capacity as a teacher leader and had no direct teaching responsibilities.

There were several limitations of the study that included nonrandom selection, low and disproportionate sample numbers, and the lack of differentiation of the teacher leaders' subject areas, departments, and grade level. All the respondents who were asked to complete the survey were very cooperative and helpful in providing opinions about their jobs and the overall value of using teacher leaders at all levels in public schools.

The core competencies of all groups were rank ordered, and significant differences were calculated using the Mann Whitney test of significance. The findings indicated that the top core competencies of importance to the *teacher leader coaches* were *mentoring and coaching* teachers and staff, *leading and motivating* teachers and staff, *improving curriculum and instruction*, and *understanding school data* (see table 2.1).

Almost all coaches rated *mentoring and coaching* a top score of 5 for importance and the mean average of all the teacher leader coaches was 4.84. Several comments by the coaches indicated that these areas were their primary responsibility. Some coaches indicated that while understanding

Table 2.1. Rank Order of Teacher Leader Coach Core Competencies

Core Competencies	Mean
1. Mentoring and coaching	4.84
2. Leading and motivating	4.58
3. Curriculum and instruction	4.45
4. Understanding school data	4.45
5. Communicating to staff	4.36
6. Managing school change	4.09
7. Building collaboration	3.97
8. Building community relations	2.97
9. Managing resources	2.12
10. Conducting teacher evaluations	0.48

school data was important, they often had colleagues within their district that they relied upon for data interpretation and analysis.

Core competencies of *communicating to staff, managing school change, building collaboration,* and *building community relations* were also deemed important, but several teacher *leader coaches* felt these competencies were not as important as the top four, which was consistent with the ranking. The lowest ranked core competencies were *managing resources* (mean = 2.12) and *conducting teacher evaluations* (mean = .48).

These were rated very low given that most of the teacher leader coaches did not manage a budget, or had a very limited one, and did not conduct formal teacher evaluations. However, some indicated that they tend to be involved in interviewing committees in hiring new teachers and staff.

The top core competencies for the *teacher leader evaluators* were *conducting teacher evaluations, mentoring and coaching* teachers and staff, *leading and motivating teachers and staff, improving curriculum and instruction,* and *understanding school data* (see table 2.2). Several teacher leaders indicated

Table 2.2.   Rank Order of Teacher Leader Evaluator Core Competencies

Core Competencies	Mean
1. Conducting teacher evaluations	4.78
2. Mentoring and coaching	4.68
3. Curriculum and instruction	4.40
4. Understanding school data	4.38
5. Leading and motivating	4.35
6. Managing resources	4.18
7. Building collaboration	4.13
8. Communicating to staff	3.97
9. Managing school change	3.92
10. Building community relations	3.20

that it was critical that they were proficient in performing teacher evaluations for compliance reasons as well as giving summative feedback for continuous improvement of the teachers.

The core competencies of *communicating to staff, managing school change, building collaboration,* and *building community relations* were also deemed important by the teacher leader evaluators and were similar in ranking as the teacher leader coaches. The main differences between the groups were that the teacher leader evaluators valued the core competencies of *managing resources* and *conducting teacher evaluations* ($p < .01$).

This is consistent with the teacher leader evaluator job responsibilities. For example, many of the teacher leader evaluators were department chairs or program coordinators and had responsibilities of managing a budget and were more involved in managing human resources such as hiring, professional development, succession planning, discipline, and terminations.

Some indicators of the study suggest that if a teacher leader is not managing a budget or evaluating teachers and staff, then the two core competencies of managing resources and conducting teacher evaluations are not relevant. This illustrates the difference between teacher leaders who are in a support role versus teacher leaders who are more in a quasi-administrative leadership role.

Table 2.3. Comparison of Core Competencies between Teacher Coaches and Teacher Evaluators

Core Competencies	Teacher Leader Coaches			Teacher Leader Evaluators		
	Mean	Median	S.D.	Mean	Median	S.D.
Mentoring and coaching	4.84	5	2.41	4.68	5	.08
Leading and motivating	4.58	5	1.82	4.35	4	.08
Improving curriculum/instruction	4.45	4	2.14	4.40	4	.11
Managing resources	*2.12	2	2.00	4.18	4	.11
Building collaboration	3.97	4	2.83	4.13	4	.11
Managing change	4.09	4	2.76	3.92	4	.11
Communicating to teachers/staff	4.36	4	1.80	3.97	4	.13
Conducting teacher evaluations	*0.48	0	1.84	4.78	5	.07
Understanding school data	4.45	5	0.90	4.38	4	.08
Building community relations	2.97	3	1.95	3.20	3	.16

*p < .01

It appears that *teacher leader coaches* tend to be more prevalent in elementary schools and *teacher leader evaluators* are more common in high schools. Further the core competencies could easily be broken into two categories of functions performed by an effective teacher leader. These two categories are *capacities* and *practices* of teacher leaders.

Capacity includes the ability to work well with colleagues and to be effective problem solvers, all seen as important to building leadership capacity. Of the ten core competencies in the study, these capacities include *understanding and using data, managing change, managing resources, improving curriculum and instruction,* and *building collaboration.*

What teacher leaders actually do can be called *practices.* These are functions and activities that are quasi-administrative in function. Of the ten core competencies, these are *mentoring and coaching, leading and motivating, building community and staff relationships,* and *conducting teacher evaluations.*

Helping all teacher leaders develop these core competencies appears to be beneficial as indicated by the teacher leaders in this study. Figure 2.2 provides a crosswalk between the competencies, the *Teacher Leader Model Standards,* and ISLLC standards. The next chapter will discuss each *Teacher Leader Model Standard* and function as it is related to the ISLLC standards and the competences and skills necessary to be an effective teacher leader.

Teacher Leader Core Competencies	Model Teacher Leader Standards	ISLLC Standards
Mentoring and coaching teachers	1, 3, 4, 6, 7	1-6
Leading and motivating	1, 3, 4, 6, 7	1-6
Improving curriculum and instruction	1, 4, 6	1-4
Managing resources	1, 2, 3, 4, 5, 6	1-4
Building collaboration	1, 3, 4, 6	1-5
Managing school change	1, 4, 6	1-4
Communicating to staff	1, 3, 4, 6	1-5
Conducting teacher evaluations	1, 2, 3, 4, 5, 6, 7	1-6
Understanding school data	1, 2, 4, 5, 6	1-4
Building community relations	1, 4, 6, 7	1-6

Figure 2.2. Crosswalk between the Core Competencies, the *Teacher Leader Model Standards* and the ISLLC Standards.

SUMMARY

The literature contains many examples of studies outlining the roles, responsibilities, capacities, and traits of teacher leaders. Leadership takes on a new meaning when attached to the words *teacher leader.* What may be different is how the influence of the *teacher leader* is accepted by the principal and the faculty.

Teacher leaders gain acceptance by their exercise of leadership capacities that influence and directly impact instruction in the classrooms of the school. Ten core competencies were identified as *capacities* and *practices* of effective teacher leaders. The study by Tomal and Wilhite (2014) outlined how practicing teacher leaders correlated these core competencies to teacher leader research.

CASE STUDY

Literacy Coach Entry Plan

You have been assigned as the new grade level teacher leader literacy coach for the intermediate (3–5) grades. The principal has asked you to write an entry plan for your new role. Consider the roles and responsibilities described in the literature.

Include the following in your description: your specific role, the context of your coaching responsibilities, your coaching qualities, content area or grade level, and anything else to better understand what you do or plan to do as a coach in your school. Consider this document as a way of justifying your position as a coach. The final format can be a brochure or a one-page handout, or any other creative way you choose to present your description.

EXERCISES AND DISCUSSION QUESTIONS

1. Research the literature about effective *coaching* and *mentoring* in teacher leadership.
2. What are the most effective characteristics of an effective *coach* or *mentor* mentioned in the literature?
3. Define the differences and similarities between *coaching* and *mentoring*.
4. Conduct your own study of teacher leaders by interviewing your colleagues to ask what core competencies are important in an effective teacher leader.
5. Formulate recommendations that you would make to your school district about how to build leadership *capacity* through teacher leadership.
6. What should occur at the building level and at the district level to support movement toward teacher leadership?

REFERENCES

Ackerman, R. and Mackenzie, S. (2006). Uncovering teacher leadership. *Educational Leadership, 63*(8), 66–70.

Anderson, K. (2004). The nature of teacher leadership in schools as reciprocal influences between teacher leaders and principals. *School Effectiveness and School Improvement, 15*(1), 97–113.

Barth, R. (2001). Teacher Leader. *Phi Delta Kappa, 82*(6), 443–449.

Beachum, F. and Dentith, A. (2004). Teacher leaders creating cultures of school renewal and transformation. *The Educational Forum, 68*(3), 276–286.

Bauer, S., Haydel, J., and Cody, C. (2003). *Cultivating teacher leadership for school improvement.* Paper presented at the Annual Meeting of the Midsouth Educational Research Association.

Bowman, R. (2004). Teachers as Leaders. *The Clearing House: Journal of Educational Strategies, Issues and Ideas, 77*(5), 187–189.

Bye, D., Pushkar, D., and Conway, M. (2007). Motivation interest and positive affect in traditional and non-traditional undergraduate students. *Adult Education Quarterly, 57*(2), 141–158.

Crowther, F., Kaagen, S. S., Ferguson, M., and Hann, L. (2002). Developing teacher leaders: How teacher leadership enhances school success. Thousand Oaks, CA: Corwin Press.

Cuban, L. (2008). *Frogs into princes: Writings on school reform.* New York: Teachers College Press.

Danielson, C. (2007). The Many Faces of Leadership. *Educational Leadership, 65*(1), 14–19.

Dozier, T. (2007). Turning good teachers into great leaders. *Teachers as Leaders, 65*(1), 54–59.

Elmore, R. F. (2007). *School reform from the inside out: Policy, practice and performance.* Cambridge, MA: Harvard Education Press.

Futernick, K. (2007). *A possible dream: Retaining California's teachers so all students learn.* Sacramento, CA: California State University.

Gonzales, L. (2004). *Sustaining teacher leadership: beyond the boundaries of an enabling school culture.* Lanham, Maryland: University Press of America Inc.

Hanushek, E. and Rivkin, S. (2009). Harming the best: How schools affect the black-white achievement gap, *Journal of Policy Analysis and Management, 28*(3), 366–393.

Harris, A. and Muijs, D. (2005). *Improving schools through teacher leadership.* New York: McGraw-Hill International.

Hatch, T., White, M., and Faigenbaum, D. (2005). Expertise, credibility, and influence: How teachers can influence policy, advance research, and improved performance. *Teacher College Record, 107*(5), 1004–1035.

Herzberg, H. (2006). Learning habits and the dynamics of lifelong learning. *Studies in the Education of Adults, 38*(1), 37–47.

Jackson, C. and Bruegmann, E. (2009). Teaching students and teaching each other: The importance of peer learning for teachers, *American Economic Journal: Applied Economics*, American Economic Association, *1*(4), 85–108.

Katzenmeyer, M. and Moller, G. (2009). *Awakening the sleeping giant: helping teachers develop as leaders.* Thousand Oaks: Corwin Press.

Leithwood, K., Anderson, S., and Wahlstrom, K. (2004). *How leadership influences student learning.* New York: Wallace Foundation.

Leithwood, K. and Beatty, B. (2008). *Leading with teacher emotions in mind.* Thousand Oaks: Corwin Press.

Leithwood, K. and Jantzi, D. (2000). Principal and teacher leadership effects: A replication. *School Leadership and Management, 20*(4), 415–434.

Lieberman, J. and Walker, D. (2007). Connecting curriculum and instruction to national teaching standards. *The Educational Forum, 71*, 274–282.

Murphy, J. (2005). *Connecting teacher leadership and school improvement.* Thousand Oaks: Corwin Press.

Murphy, J., Elliott, S., Goldring, E., and Porter, A. (2006). *Learning-centered leadership: A conceptual foundation.* New York: The Wallace Foundation.

Nieto, S. (2003). *What keeps teachers going.* New York, Teachers College Press.

Papa, F., Lankford, H., and Wyckoff, J. (2003). *Great teachers and great leaders.* Retrieved [2013] from U.S. Department of Education, http://www2.ed.gov/policy/elsec/leg/blueprint/great-teachers-great leaders.pdf.

Remedios, R. and Boreham, N. (2004). Organizational learning and employee's intrinsic motivation. *Journal of Education and Work, 17*(2), 219–235.

Rivkin, S., Hanushek, E., and Kain, J. (2005). Teachers, Schools and Academic Achievement, *Econometrica,* (March) 73(2), 417–458.

Ross, J. and Gray, P. (2006). Transformational leadership and teacher commitment to organizational values: the mediating effects of collective teacher efficacy. *School Effectiveness and School Improvement, 17*(2), 179–199.

Silva, D., Gimbert, B., and Nolan, J. (2000). Sliding the doors: locking and unlocking possibilities for teacher leadership. *Teachers College Record, 102*(4), 779–804.

Spillane, J., Halverson, R., and Diamond, J. (2001). Investigating school leadership practice: A distributive perspective. *Educational Researcher, 30*(3), 23–27.

The Center for Comprehensive School Reform and Improvement (2005). "Research Brief: What does the research tell us about Teacher Leadership?" Washington, DC. http://www.centerforcsri.org/files/Center_RB_sept05.pdf.

Tickle, E., Brownlee, J., and Nailon, D. (2005). Personal epistemological beliefs and transformational leadership behaviors. *The Journal of Management Development, 24*, 1–15.

Tomal, D. and Wilhite, R. (2014). A comparison of core competencies of teacher leaders in K-12 public schools. Unpublished research study.

Wendel, F., Hoke, F., and Josekel, R. (1993). Project success: Outstanding principals speak out. *The Clearing House: Journal of Educational Strategies, Issues and Ideas, 67*(1), 52–54.

Wetig, S. (2002). *Step up or step out: Perspectives on teacher leadership.* Paper presented at the Annual Meeting of the American Educational Research Association.

York-Barr, J. and Duke, K. (2004). What do we know about teacher leadership? Findings of two decades of scholarship. *Review of Educational Research, 74*(3), 255–316.

Chapter 3

Standards Based Teacher Leadership

OBJECTIVES

At the conclusion of this chapter, you will be able to:

1. Gain an understanding of teacher leader skills, dispositions and competencies (ISLLC 6; ELCC 6; TLEC 2, 6; InTASC 4, 5, 6)
2. Understand *Teacher Leader Model Standards* (ISLLC 6; ELCC 6; TLEC 2, 6; InTASC 4, 5, 6)
3. Review the link between research and standards-based leadership (ISLLC 6; ELCC 6; TLEC 2, 7; InTASC 1, 4, 5, 6, 9, 10).
4. Understand the ISLLC leadership policy standards and the link to the *Teacher Leader Model Standards* (ISLLC 6; ELCC 6; TLEC 2, 6, In-TASC 4, 5, 6)

NATIONAL LEADERSHIP STANDARDS

For nearly two decades, the standards-based movement has shadowed students, teachers, and administrators. From test taking skills to test results, everyone rates schools based on annual test scores. There is little doubt that the accountability movement has been a challenge for the American education system. Accreditation agencies, state boards of education, politicians, and parents have demanded excellent schools. This has pushed educators to focus laser-like on the ultimate goal of educating all children who attend our schools.

One aspect of the accountability movement has helped to define and usher in a wave of reform. Reformers agree that one of the best methods to ensure excellence is better training and the establishment of national standards for the leadership in schools. Such national standards like the *Intrastate School Leaders Licensure Consortium* (ISLLC, 2011) for school leaders have led the way for setting benchmarks for the quality of the leadership skills needed in our schools.

Standards may or may not improve leadership. Yet, they are used to change and redesign higher education programs that grant endorsements or certifications for future school leaders. This chapter examines those standards for school leaders, their use in building leadership capacity, and their effectiveness for change in schools.

The standards used are the ISLLC leadership policy standards and the *Teacher Leader Model Standards.* They illustrate the skills and dispositions for effective school leadership and those roles, responsibilities, and dispositions used to transform these standards into best practices in schools. They build upon the standards of effective leadership as tailored for teacher leaders.

Building capacity for leadership means school leaders must use effective instructional practices identified in the literature and the field to improve the performance of children. It means relevant professional growth programs that develop and expand teacher pedagogy in classrooms. These instructional practices must have direct impact on the performance of students. Standards based benchmarks can help define the level of expertise needed to advance such practices in American schools.

The National Policy Board for Educational Administration (NPBEA; 2002) has been a leading voice in this area. Their policy paper states, "Educational leaders must be able to work with diverse groups and to integrate ideas to solve a common flow of problems. They must study their craft as they practice their craft, reflecting and then applying what they have learned to people and institutions and the achievement task" (p. 3).

The questions addressed by the ISLLC standards for effective leadership are these:

1. What does a leader need to know? (content knowledge)
2. What does a leader need to do? (skills and practices)
3. What are the dispositions of an effective leader? (behaviors and attributes)

The NPBEA developed the ISLLC policy standards to inform educators in the field and those in university preparation programs. They can be used as assessment tools or as teaching tools focused on content knowledge, performance skills and the attributes of successful school leaders. The ISLLC standards address 1) vision and mission, 2) teaching and learning, 3) managing systems and climate, 4) collaboration with key stakeholders, 5) ethics and integrity, and 6) larger context for education (see table 1.1).

Another set of standards that mirror the ISLLC standards is the *Educational Leadership Consortium Council* (ELCC), also a member of NPBEA. The standards prescribed by ELCC are similar in scope to those suggested by ISLLC. The ELCC standards address the same six categories as seen in the ISLLC standards with one additional category of internship experiences, which provide direct school-based opportunities to apply and practice the knowledge and skills learned in the preparation program.

Programs of educational preparation in school leadership that wish to have accreditation by the National Council for Accreditation of Teacher Education (NCATE) are required to meet these standards. The NCATE recently changed to *Council for Accreditation of Educator Preparation* (CAEP) guidelines. New CAEP guidelines are under development and will be forthcoming in future months outlining revised standards, accreditation procedures, and best practices in educator preparation.

The ISLLC and ELCC standards were not meant to be inclusive but were written to be guides or benchmarks for helping practitioners and educational leader preparation programs understand what was important for improving schools and the teaching of all children. So then how do these standards apply to the teacher leader movement and how should they be used to improve teacher leadership skills? In the next sections we will explore and expand the *Teacher Leader Model Standards* and benchmark each of the seven standards (domains) with the ISLLC leadership policy standards.

THE SEVEN TEACHER LEADER MODEL STANDARDS

Using the teacher leader core competencies identified in chapters 1 and 2, figure 3.1 illustrates a conceptual framework to help structure the examination of the link between the *Teacher Leader Model Standards* and the ISLLC leadership policy standards. This structure ties together competencies, leadership and outcomes for meaningful school improvement.

The six ISLLC standards are meant to highlight effective school leadership. The *Teacher Leader Model Standards* are meant to highlight effective teacher leader behaviors and functions. Each element or function in the standard is meant to expand on the skills identified in that standard and provide additional examples of content knowledge needed, practices, and dispositions used to describe an effective teacher leader.

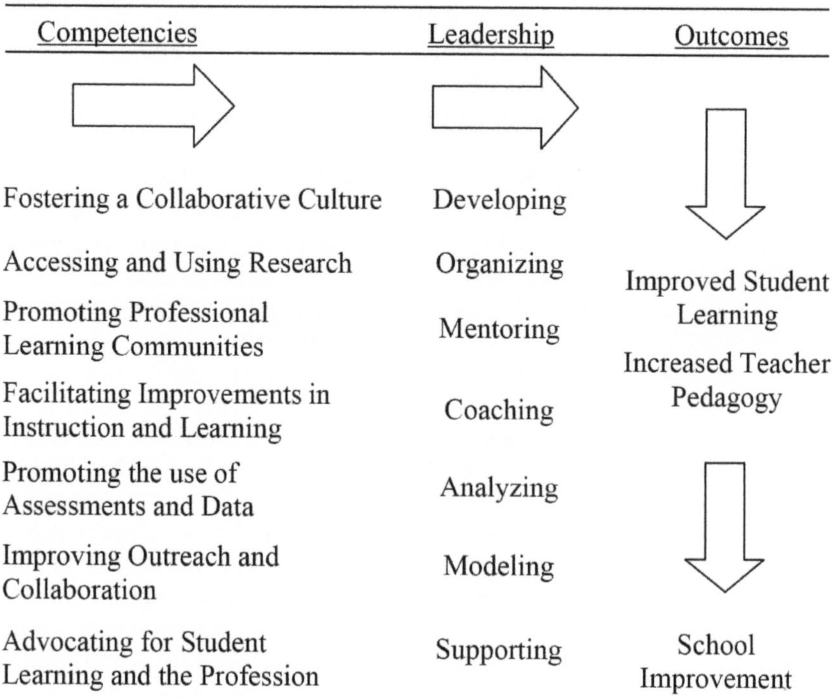

Competencies	Leadership	Outcomes

Fostering a Collaborative Culture | Developing

Accessing and Using Research | Organizing

Improved Student Learning

Promoting Professional Learning Communities | Mentoring

Increased Teacher Pedagogy

Facilitating Improvements in Instruction and Learning | Coaching

Promoting the use of Assessments and Data | Analyzing

Improving Outreach and Collaboration | Modeling

Advocating for Student Learning and the Profession | Supporting | School Improvement

Figure 3.1.   Framework for Teacher Leadership

Source: Based on an interpretation of the Teacher Leader Model Standards, 2010. Teacher Leadership Exploratory Consortium. R. Wilhite, 2013.

Standard 1: Advocating for Student Learning and the Profession

Understands the principles of adult learning and knows how to develop a collaborative culture of collective responsibility in the school. Uses this knowledge to promote an environment of collegiality, trust, and respect that focuses on continuous improvement in instruction and learning.

Function a: Uses group processes, works collaboratively, manages conflict, promotes change—ISLLC standards 1C, 3C, 3D.

In the school setting, the effective teacher leader will use *distributive leadership* to create and implement school improvement projects, create small study groups to improve instruction, and will collaborate in the development and writing of curriculum and lesson plans. *Distributive leadership* allows for shared responsibilities to balance the load of the team goals. It also builds within each team member a capacity for leadership and shared decision making. There are times in this process that conflict will arise among the team members and the teacher leader will attempt to problem solve involving all members of the team or group.

The teacher leader will manage conflict using conflict resolution strategies to effectively promote staff and faculty well-being while promoting a climate of respect and trust. The purpose of this function is to improve student learning and enhance meaningful change in classroom practices and instruction.

Function b: Models effective listening skills, leads discussions, mediates, and identifies personal and group goals—ISLLC standards 1C, 5B.

Modeling is one of the most effective strategies teacher leaders have in their repertoire of skills. Using the principles of self-awareness, reflective practices, and complete transparency, the teacher leader becomes a guide for the others in the team, the grade level, or the group. This requires the techniques of advancing shared goals, leading brainstorming activities that result in the implementation of goals and improved professional learning for all involved.

The modeling used by the teacher leader relies heavily on the personality of that leader. This takes personal integrity and ethical behavior that promotes credibility in actions and in words. The purpose of this function is to advance shared goals and to develop professional growth in all participants.

Function c: Uses facilitation skills to create trust, develop collective wisdom, and build ownership—ISLLC 2A.

When working with a group of colleagues in developing shared goals, it is important to have a climate in which it is safe to share ideas, have spirited discussions without conflict, and to maintain collegiality and respect. The effective teacher leader will use activities, behaviors, and actions that sustain a culture of collaboration while maintaining trust and encouraging high expectations for all involved. The purpose of this function is to have team members develop actions that support and improve student learning.

Function d: Creates an inclusive culture where diverse ideas and thoughts are encouraged and welcomed—ISLLC standard 5C.

The teacher leader behavior fosters a climate of openness for all involved. The teacher leader encourages acceptance of a wide variety of ideas and solutions to challenges while maintaining respect for the thought processes of all participants. Diverse ideas are encouraged and accepted in a spirit of shared appreciation of ideas. The purpose of this function is to have equity in all ideas presented as a norm in the group process.

Function e: Uses knowledge of diverse ethnicities, cultures, and languages to pro-mote positive interactions among colleagues—ISLLC standard 4B.

The effective teacher leader will promote understanding and appre-ciation of each colleague's background to develop capacity in the group process. In the school setting, it is important for faculty and staff to under-stand the importance of the culture in which they work. Everyone brings a diverse cultural, social, and intellectual background to the challenges exhibited in schools and to the learning issues of the students we teach. The purpose of this function is to capitalize on these cultural and social differences as strengths in the problem solving processes.

Standard 2: Accessing and Using Research to Improve Practice and Student Learning

Understands how research creates new knowledge, informs policies and practices and improves teaching and learning. Models and facilitates the use of systematic inquiry as a critical component of teachers' ongoing learning and development.

Function a: Assists in accessing and using research to select and analysis instruc-tional strategies that improve student learning—ISLLC standard 4A.

In the school setting teacher leaders should assist colleagues in ac-cessing, collecting, and analyzing data that focuses on best practices in instructional delivery. This can be done through small group processing, one on one, or in teams of teachers. It can be done by common content area, by grade level, such as all first grade teachers, or done by grade spans such as all primary teachers in a team.

The teacher leader is a key player in helping colleagues to locate best practices in the literature, framing a common approach to the analysis of this research, and helping to frame the discussions about how these strategies may work in the classroom. The purpose of this function is to impact the direct delivery of instruction in the classroom on a day-to-day basis improving the learning conditions for students.

Function b: Facilitates analysis of student learning data, creates a collaborative cul-ture of inquiry focused on results that improve student learning—ISLLC standards 1E, 3A, 4A.

The effective teacher leader sets a tone and a culture of professional best practices in the collection, analysis, and evaluation of data. The focus is on student test results and how to improve learning. The teacher leader will assist and collaborate with colleagues to monitor the student data, evaluate the results, review student progress, and formulate plans to in-crease student performance.

It is not uncommon for the teacher leader to chair a committee of teach-ers in a systematic approach to analysis and interpretation of student test results on a continuous basis. This systematic approach provides feedback to the classroom teacher about instructional strategies that are working and are not working with the goal in mind of increasing student performance levels on local tests, standardized tests, and in overall classroom performance outcomes. The focus of the function is improvement of teaching and learning.

Function c: Supports colleagues in consultation with higher learning institutions and other organizations in researching crucial educational issues—ISLLC standard 4D.

The teacher leader must be aware of the partnerships within the community that support and assist with data collection and analysis. Higher education is a natural resource for data collection and analysis techniques. If there is a climate and an expectation for collaboration, then it is a natural ongoing process for the teacher leader to build on this capacity for research engagement. The goal is to build and sustain positive relationships with community organizations and partners. The focus of this function is to build a network for ongoing and sustained collaborative partnerships.

Function d: Teaches and supports colleagues in the collection, analysis, and communication of data form their classrooms to improve teaching and learning—ISLLC standard 1B.

It should be part of the school vision and mission to continually want to improve. An effective technique in school improvement is data analysis of each classroom student performance. Such analysis needs guidance and support. This is a natural role for the teacher leader who can model and teach colleagues how to efficiently collect student performance data, analysis such data, and effectively communicate this analysis to parents, students, and colleagues.

Such analysis should not only match the vision and mission of the school improvement process but more importantly meet the needs of students. The purpose of this function is to place emphasis on the ongoing improvement of instructional practices and the learning by all students.

Standard 3: Promoting Professional Learning for Continuous Improvement

Understands the evolving nature of teaching and learning, the established and emerging technologies, and school community. Uses this knowledge to promote, design, and facilitate job-embedded professional learning aligned with school improvement goals.

Function a: Collaborates with colleagues and administrators to plan professional learning that is team-based, job-embedded, sustained over time, and aligned with content standards, and linked to school and district improvement goals—ISLLC standards 1A, 2F.

Function b: Uses information about adult learning to respond to the diverse learning needs of colleagues by identifying promoting and facilitating varied and differentiated professional learning—ISLLC standards 1A, 2F.

The leadership skills needed for the teacher leader in these areas are in building shared vision and mission with the stakeholders of the school. In collaboration with the school administration, the teacher leader should assist in the development of leadership capacity among colleagues with the purpose of improvement of student performance and learning.

This could be in the form of professional learning communities, small teams of teachers by content area, grade level, or by team. All of the professional development training and learning activities should be meaningful, directly tied to the classroom practices, and provide for direct linkage to the school or the district improvement goals. The purpose of these functions is to build organizational capacity as a professional learning community.

Function c: Facilitates professional learning among colleagues—ISLLC standards 1D, 2A.
Function d: Identifies and uses appropriate technologies to promote collaboration and differentiated professional learning—ISLLC standards 1D, 2A.

The teacher leader can be a key player in developing a culture of collaboration, trust, and high expectations in the professional development activities of colleagues. A teacher leader can promote, encourage, support, and facilitate planning of those training activities that best meet the needs of the teachers and also the goals of the school and district improvement goals.

The purpose of these functions is to encourage the teacher leader to use skills and knowledge to identify, articulate, plan, and help implement those training activities that best meet teacher instructional needs and the learning goals of the school with a focus on an ongoing supported process of professional growth for all faculty and staff.

Function e: Works with colleagues to collect, analyze, and disseminate data related to the quality of professional learning and its effect on teaching and student learning—ISLLC standard 1B.

The leadership traits needed for this function focus on modeling and the teaching of effective data collection strategies. The teacher leader needs to assist colleagues in assessing data in an effective manner related to the individual teacher classroom and school improvement goals.

The purpose of this function is to encourage the teacher leader to assist in the development of effective instruments and procedures to collect data about best training activities that promote individual teacher growth, effectiveness of practice in the field with a direct relationship to improved student learning.

Function f: Advocates for sufficient preparation, time, and support for colleagues to work in teams to engage in job-embedded professional learning—ISLLC standards 2G, 6B.

One of the primary roles of a teacher leader is advocacy. In this leadership function, teacher leaders should be the voice of colleagues in seeking an adequate amount of time to engage in and collaborate about activities and training that enhance professional growth and collegial learning.

The teacher leader should seek to maximize the time allocated for effective daily instruction. Teachers need time to implement those instructional strategies they have researched and analyzed for student learning. They should also act to influence the local administration, the district leadership, and the school board to provide for adequate time for teachers to collaborate and plan together.

In the larger context, teacher leaders can also be advocates and the voice of teachers at the state and federal levels in policy development that impacts the day-to-day instruction in the classroom. They can have a direct influence on the laws and statutes written that impact teachers and students in their schools. The purpose of this function is to encourage teacher leaders to act in their important role as advocates for colleagues and students they serve.

Function g: Provides constructive feedback to colleagues to strengthen teaching practices and improve student learning—ISLLC standard 2F.

In the school setting, this is one of several critical leadership functions a teacher leader performs to improve the instruction and learning in the classrooms of the school. The teacher leader can coach colleagues by providing examples of exemplary practices and techniques. They can lead colleagues to relevant research in the improvement of instruction.

The teacher leader can also model teaching practices for colleagues. They can provide time for guided dialogue and reflection about teaching practices. The purpose of this function is to encourage teacher leaders to understand and support their colleagues and at the same time build the capacity of the organization for sustained change.

Function h: Uses information about emerging education, economic, and social trends in planning and facilitating professional learning—ISLLC standard 6A, 6B, 6C.

Understanding the larger context of the role they play in schools is critical to success as a teacher leader. They must act in the roles of advocates, coaches, and mentors to fellow colleagues at the local, state, and national levels to influence and improve the educational environment. They must continually reflect upon best practices, analyze current trends in educational practices, demonstrate best teaching practices, and anticipate future change.

This is a complex role. It is new to many of them as they enter the teacher leader ranks. The purpose of the function is to remind and encourage teacher leaders to remain current and up-to-date in their own learning so that they can provide for the most effective learning opportunities for their colleagues.

Standard 4: Facilitating Improvements in Instruction and Student Learning

Demonstrates a deep understanding of the teaching and learning processes and uses this knowledge to advance the professional skills of colleagues by being a continuous learner and modeling reflective practice based on student results. Works collaboratively with colleagues to endure instructional practices are aligned to a shared vision, mission, and goals.

Function a: Facilitates the collection, analysis, and use of classroom and school-based data to identify opportunities to improve curriculum, instruction, assessment, school organization, and school culture—ISLCC standards 2B, 2D, 2I

This is the first function in the teacher leader standards that focuses on supervision and monitoring of instruction. The teacher leader is charged with the responsibility to monitor and evaluate effective instructional programs. In this supervisory role, the teacher leader has two pathways to accomplish this leadership function—informal supervision and formal evaluative supervision.

In the informal role, the teacher leader acts as a coach and assists colleagues in the improvement of instructional practices by modeling, mentoring, and assisting teachers in the writing and implementation of best practices. In the formal role, the teacher leader evaluates the teacher in the classroom in the delivery of instruction as well as the monitoring and collection of student performance data.

Since the teacher leader movement is growing in popularity across the nation, there are two schools of thoughts about the formal and informal supervisory role of teacher leaders. Some states like Illinois have added a supervisory/evaluative function to the teacher leader endorsement. The teacher leader must have taken formal evaluation training and had course work in supervision and the evaluation of teachers.

Other states like Ohio, Louisiana, Georgia, and Texas have gone the informal mentoring and coaching route for the teacher leader avoiding formal teacher evaluation training. This comes closer to the true definition of a teacher leader as reviewed in the literature. The teacher leader is viewed as a collegial and collaborative partner working with fellow teachers.

Regardless of which pathway taken, the effective teacher leader uses coaching and mentoring techniques to help colleagues improve their instructional practices in the classroom. These mentoring and coaching techniques involve facilitation of data collection, documented steps in the analysis of student data, and assistance in identifying student strengths and weaknesses in learning.

Based on this data collection, teacher leaders assist teachers in improving curriculum, making changes in instructional delivery, and enhanced lesson writing. Teacher learners also use modeling strategies by visiting classrooms and teaching for their colleagues. The purpose of this function is to create a rigorous approach to improvement of instructional practices.

Function b: Engages in reflective dialogue with colleagues based on observations of instruction, student work, and assessment data and helps make connections to research-based effective practices—ISLLC standard 3C.

An effective strategy in any profession is reflection about practice. The teacher leader should model reflective practice and assist colleagues in personal anecdotal documentation of their own practices. A system of analysis should be in place where teachers can analysis instructional practices and make decisions about their own personal effectiveness based on student data collected and analyzed.

The focus of this reflective practice should be on quality of instruction and the student learning in the classroom on a daily basis. The purpose of this function is to remind and encourage teacher leaders about the importance of quality in the instructional program tied to the connections in the literature and the field about effective and continuous improvement.

Function c: Supports colleagues' individual and collective reflection and professional growth by serving in roles such as mentor, coach, and content facilitator—ISLLC standards 2A, 3D.

If a climate of collaborative trust has been established, then the teacher leader can develop distributive leadership among colleagues. By serving as a teacher, a student advocate, and guide, the teacher leader can encourage, develop, and assist in building strong personal relationships with colleagues. These relationships can encourage risk taking by teachers to try new and innovative methods to improve instruction and analyze results.

Teachers can use the teacher leader to reference best practices, find connections in the research about best practices, and make informed decisions about their own professional growth. The purpose of this function is to remind teacher leaders of the importance of their role in supporting and facilitating shared leadership among fellow teachers.

Function d: Serves as a team leader to harness skills, expertise, and knowledge of colleagues to address curricular expectations and student learning needs—ISLLC standards 2C, 3D.

In a climate where continuous improvement is promoted and practiced, the teacher leader acts as the guide or the team leader in identifying the skills and dispositional strengths of the team members. The focus of this leadership skill is to build the capacity of the team to address instructional issues that impede learning and those that foster learning. The purpose of this function is to remind teacher leaders of the important of team building and the leadership role of maximizing strengths and minimizing individual colleague weaknesses.

Function e: Uses knowledge of existing and emerging technologies to guide colleagues in helping students skillfully and appropriately navigate the universe of knowledge available on the Internet, use social media to promote collaborative learning, and connect people and resources around the globe—ISLLC standards 2H, 3B.

The children of the digital age are more comfortable, knowledgeable, and literate in *tech bites* of visual and audio cues than in printed words. The challenge for teachers is to harness this knowledge and develop *tech savvy kids* who can navigate and use the internet as a tool and as social media. In our students' world, all use of technology needs to be interactive. This notion is supported by the concept of an engaged learner. Not only must we teach students how to use technology to enhance learning, but we also need to teach students how to use technology appropriately.

The leadership skills needed by the teacher leader to accomplish these goals requires an understanding of best practices in technology classroom use and in helping colleagues grow personally in the use of technology and how to use technology as an effective teaching tool.

An excellent source for technology best practices is the *Technology Standards for School Administrators* (TSSA; see appendix C). The *TSSA Collaborative* has facilitated the development of a national consensus on what PK–12 administrators should know and be able to do to optimize the effective use of technology.

This is a useful reference tool for teacher leaders to utilize with teams of teachers to review and develop classroom strategies that link technology use to standards. The purpose of this function is to remind teacher leaders of the importance of understanding the use of appropriate technologies in the school setting.

Function f: Promotes instructional strategies that address issues of diversity and equity in the classroom and ensures that individual student learning needs remain the central focus of instruction—ISLLC standards 2C, 2F, 5C.

Central to the function of any school is to develop a deep understanding and appreciation of our cultural and ethnic differences. This focus on diversity is even more important in the changing world in which we live. Our students come to us from diverse backgrounds and cultures with multiple languages that impact the delivery of instruction. If we are to maintain the central focus on student learning, then the leadership skills of the teacher leader should be guiding colleagues in developing a classroom climate that promotes diverse values, languages, and learning styles.

Teacher leaders play a vital role in establishing this culture of acceptance of shared values. The teacher leader must exhibit personal understanding of differentiated learning and help colleagues understand how to plan this into daily lessons. It is a matter of capacity building once again. Teacher leaders must encourage colleagues to research best practices in the teaching of all learners. The purpose of this function is to remind and encourage teacher leaders of the central role they play in advancing equity in education for all learners.

Standard 5: Promoting the Use of Assessments and Data for School and District Improvement

Knowledgeable about current research on classroom and school-based data and the design and selection of appropriate formative and summative assessment methods. Shares knowledge and collaborates with colleagues in the use of assessment and other data to make informed decisions that improve learning for all students and to inform school and district improvement strategies.

Function a: Increases capacity of colleagues to identify and use multiple assessment tools aligned to state and local standards—ISLLC standard 2F.

During the process of continuous review of classroom data, the teacher leader role is to build a process for locating the best practices in instruction and to locate multiple measures for identifying student strengths and weaknesses. These measures should also provide feedback to the teachers about how the instruction is meeting the goals of the curriculum or the program taught.

The school improvement plan should also provide a framework for the measures that are most important to meeting the goals of the school. The teacher leader's role is to gather this information, share it with teachers, and help them to make sense of the data generated. Then support and assist colleagues in applying the results discovered from the review to the actual practices in the classroom. The purpose of this function is to build knowledge and skills among teachers for continuous improvement in instructional delivery for increased student performance.

Function b: Collaborates with colleagues in the design, implementation, scoring, and interpretation of student data to improve educational practices and student learning— ISLLC standards 1D, 2E, 5A.

Inherent in this function is the issue of accountability for improved student learning. As seen in earlier functions, the teacher leader provides a culture of collaboration and accountability where shared information results in good decision making. Part of this process is modeling by the teacher leader to guide and teach colleagues how to score tests, how to interpret scores, and how to use the results in the change process of instructional delivery and methodology.

The goal of this process is a constant and sustained improvement process. Ideally this occurs daily but at a minimum weekly when lesson plans are reviewed and updated to meet the needs of the learners. The purpose of this function is to remind teacher leaders of the importance of modeling and collaborating with colleagues to achieve optimal teaching results for improved student performance.

Function c: Creates a climate of trust and critical reflection in order to engage colleagues in challenging conversations about student learning data that lead to solutions to identified issues—ISLLC standards 2A, 5B.

Teacher leaders are the guides to the process of reflections and critical conversations. It is the conversations that generate solutions to challenges in student performance levels. The climate created for collaboration supports a balanced and fair approach to sharing information and problem solving. The teacher leader establishes a process that is fair, ethical and relevant to colleagues.

Often the conversations can become heated and teacher egos get in the way of solutions. The leadership skills of the teacher leader are essential to making sure that the process works and remains open to all participants. The conversations should remain focused on student learning and not on individual teacher personalities. The teacher leader can guide the discussion in such a way that outcome based problem solving becomes the focus. The purpose of this function is to remind teacher leaders that an assessment system based on fair and equable approaches to accountability are essential to school improvement.

Function d: Works with colleagues to use assessment and data findings to promote changes in instructional practices or organizational structures to improve student learning—ISLLC standard 1B.

The role of the teacher leader in establishing the correct use of data is critical to the relevance of that data. If the teacher leader has established a climate for inquiry, then these findings can be used in the change process for improvement. Essential to the process established by the teacher leader in team building is the understanding of how the change process influences the teachers' personal and profession lives.

If the ultimate goal is to improve student learning and this should be the goal, then the teacher leader must establish a framework that works for all involved. The purpose of this function is help teacher leaders establish a systematic review process containing relevant and appropriate assessment instruments, methods of collection, methods of analysis, and methods of implementing results into the day to day teaching of the teachers.

Standard 6: Improving Outreach and Collaboration with Families and Community

Understands that families, cultures, and communities have a significant impact on educational processes and student learning. Works with colleagues to promote ongoing systematic collaboration with families, community members, business and community leaders, and other stakeholders to improve the educational system and expand opportunities for student learning.

Function a: Uses knowledge and understanding of the different backgrounds, ethnicities, cultures, and languages in the school community to promote effective interactions among colleagues, families, and the larger community—ISLLC standards 3C, 4B.

This is an important function for faculty and staff in any school. This is also a function that can be easily overlooked or unattended if not carefully planned and monitored. The teacher leader can play a key role in helping to implement this function in a school. By working directly with colleagues in establishing a climate and culture of diversity in the classroom, in the curriculum, and in the day to day operations of the school, the teacher leader can support and provide outreach to community members as a student and family advocate.

Most importantly, the teacher leader must be able to understand the community they serve and understand that safety and welfare are key factors in positive student performance. They must be able to articulate the backgrounds of the students and families served. They must be able to promote and facilitate positive interactions between their colleagues and community stakeholders. The purpose of this key function is to remind teacher leaders that they are important role models in outreach to their community.

Function b: Models and teaches effective communication and collaboration skills with families and other stakeholders focused on attaining equitable achievement for students of all backgrounds and circumstances—ISLLC standard 4C.

The building of sustained and positive relationships with families and community members is essential to school success. How a school is perceived in the community promotes a positive climate for students and teachers. Community members need to know and understand their schools. The role of teacher leaders as advocates and spokespersons for the faculty and students helps to establish a positive rapport between the school and community members. The purpose of this function is to highlight and remind teacher leaders that they are key advocates for the climate of their school and in helping the community to understand that climate for learning.

Function c: Facilitates colleagues' self-examination of their own understandings of community culture and diversity and how they can develop culturally responsive strategies to enrich the educational experiences of students and achieve high levels of learning for all students—ISLLC standard 5C.

In their role as liaisons to the community and leaders in the faculty, teacher leaders can assist colleagues with understanding the culture and norms of the families they serve. They also can assist and collaborate with colleagues in the development of enriching curriculum that promotes and enhances acceptance and awareness of cultural diversity in the students taught. By helping teachers with writing curriculum and planning programs for high expectations, teacher leaders help to achieve the goal of community outreach.

Teacher leaders provide the framework for work teams where teacher and student backgrounds are celebrated. These celebrations of differences used to reach common goals of learning for all students are critical components for student and school success. The purpose of this function is to remind teacher leaders of their role in framing an enriching and diverse culture for their school understood by the larger community.

Function d: Develops a shared understanding among colleagues of the diverse educational needs of families and the community—ISLCC standard 4A.

As teacher leaders work in teams of colleagues in the systematic review of performance analysis, focus should also be on the unique needs of the learners and families in the community. There should be time to communicate and share anecdotal information about different backgrounds, the varying ethnic groups in the school and the different languages of the students.

All of these variables need to be factored into the day-to-day operations, the focus of the curriculum, and the unique needs of the students served. The focus should be on reaching a common goal of educating all learners. The purpose of this function is to remind teacher leaders of the importance of the work groups and the need for sharing important and relevant student and family demographic data and the impact on the delivery of instruction in the school.

Function e: Collaborates with families, communities, and colleagues to develop comprehensive strategies to address the diverse educational needs of families and the community—ISLLC standard 4C.

The building of positive and sustained relationships with families and community members is essential to school mission. Schools are lighthouses in the communities they serve and as such should be places of acceptance and learning for all community members. They should reflect and celebrate the rich heritage of the community.

Part of any school improvement plan should be goals centered on community involvement. The teacher leader can serve a role in the implementation of such goals. The teacher leader can help to build internal structures in the school that recognize and foster diversity. The teacher leader can serve as a spokesperson and liaison for the larger community in drawing them into the school for ancillary and support services. The purpose of this function is to highlight the important role teacher leaders serve in outreach to families and community members.

Standard 7: Promoting Professional Learning for Continuous Improvement

Understands how educational policy is made at the local, state, and national level as well as the roles of school leaders, boards of education, legislators, and other stakeholders in formulating those policies. Uses knowledge to advocate for student needs and for practices that support effective teaching and increase student learning, and serves as an individual of influence and respect within the school, community, and profession.

Function a: Shares information with colleagues within and/or beyond the district regarding how local, state, and national trends and policies can impact classroom practices and expectations for student learning—ISLLC standard 6C.

The teacher leader must be a continuous learner. In this role, a teacher leader is expected to be able to share leading edge instructional techniques, classroom best practices, and have access to research supporting these practices. Sharing this knowledge is an important role of the successful teacher leader.

Teacher leaders are master teachers in every sense of the word. They not only can locate, articulate, and share best practices, they model them for their colleagues both inside and outside the district and community they serve. The purpose of this function is to highlight the importance of the teacher leader connections to emerging trends and current practices that impact student learning.

Function b: Works with colleagues to identify and use research to advocate for teaching and learning processes that meet the needs of all students—ISLLC standards 5D, 6A, 6B.

In their role as sharers of emerging trends and practices, teacher leaders are expected to advocate and promote best practices. They are voices for students and colleagues. They must create an environment of discourse focusing on research that supports efficient and effective teaching methodology. The purpose of this function is to help teacher leaders understand the critical role they serve as advocates for their colleagues and students for best practices.

Function c: Collaborates with colleagues to select appropriate opportunities to advocate for the rights and/or needs of students, to secure additional resources within the building or district that support student learning, and to communicate effectively with targeted audiences such as parents and community members—ISLCC 5D, 5E, 6B.

Teacher leaders are in roles where they can influence decision making. By virtue of their connection to colleagues, their expertise in best practices, and their role as advocates, they can promote what is in the best interest of their learners and their colleagues. They have a responsibility to act to influence decision making in polices, resource management, and equity of learning.

They are key spokespersons on behalf of the rights of their learners and their colleagues. They are participants in key committees in the district and state levels to advocate on behalf what is in the best interest for all learners. They speak to parents, community members, legislative committees, community partners, and policy makers about the needs of learners. They advocate for the goal of educating all learners. The purpose of this function is to remind teacher leaders of their role as advocate cheerleaders of education.

Function d: Advocates for access to professional resources, including financial support and human and other material resources that allow colleagues to spend significant time learning about effective practices and developing a professional learning community focused don school improvement goals—ISLLC standard 6B.

As read in previous functions, the teacher leader has a key role in equality access for all learners and colleagues. They are spokespersons for resource management, for open access to research that can make a difference in teaching practice. They are key players in the development of professional learning communities in their schools advocating for and leading their communities in pursuit of quality learning for all students.

They continually act to influence policy makers and leaders who can deliver needed resources to the classroom. The purpose of this function is to ensure that teacher leaders clearly understand their role in speaking up for colleagues and students whenever and wherever necessary.

Function e: Represents and advocates for the profession in contexts outside of the classroom—ISLLC standards 5D, 5E, 6B, 6C.

Teacher leaders have a moral and ethical responsibility to represent their colleagues and their collective students. They are spokespersons, advocates, leaders, and cheerleaders for the right to an education in our democratic society. They work tirelessly to make a difference in the lives of those they represent. Teacher leaders act to influence and promote social justice in every opportunity they have. The purpose of this function is to remind teacher leaders of their responsibility and their moral obligation to advocate for their learners, their colleagues, and for the profession they represent.

SUMMARY

In this chapter, the *Teacher Leader Model Standards* were outlined and examples given to illustrate the skills and competencies needed to become an effective teacher leader. The ISLLC standards were provided to add depth and dimension to the teacher leader functions within the *Teacher Leader Model Standards*.

The teacher leader adds leadership capacity to the school setting. They can mentor, advocate, coach, and are spokespersons for the students and colleagues in their schools. Effective teacher leaders demonstrate skills that support the vision, mission, and goals of their school. It is also evident that teacher leaders serve an important role in support of the teaching profession.

CASE STUDY

Teacher Leader—School District 100

You are applying for a teacher leader position in one of the middle schools. In the application you are asked write a two-page response to the following questions: "Reflect on the *Teacher Leader Model Standards* as they relate to instructional leadership roles, responsibilities, and accountability to improve teacher practices and student learning. Also, assess and explain your domains of strength and where you wish to grow."

EXERCISES AND DISCUSSION QUESTIONS

1. How will you determine if you have acquired the skills and dispositions needed to meet each of the *Teacher Leader Model Standards*?
2. Using your school or district as an example, what key assessments are in place to determine student performance levels in reading and mathematics? Why were these chosen as measurements?
3. What strategies could be used in team building to create an inclusive climate where all viewpoints are heard and respected?
4. Research effective leadership methods that foster collaboration and sharing among colleagues.
5. What strategies are identified in research as effective community partnership tools to promote involvement of stakeholders in schools?

REFERENCES

Educational Leadership Consortium Council, ELCC standards. (2002). Washington, DC, National Policy Board for Educational Administration (NPBEA).

Interstate School Leaders Licensure Consortium, ISLLC standards. (2011). Washington DC, Interstate School Leaders Licensure Consortium of Chief State School Officers.

Technology Standards for School Administrators. (2002). TSSA Framework, Standards, and Performance Indicators 4, International Society for Technology in Education (ISTE).

Teacher Leader Model Standards. (2010). Teacher Leader Exploratory Consortium. Washington, DC. www.teacherleaderstandards.org/

Chapter 4

Selecting, Coaching, and Mentoring

OBJECTIVES

At the conclusion of this chapter you will be able to:

1. Understand principles and techniques of interviewing and selecting employees (ELCC 3.1, ISLLC 1, 3, TLEC 1, 3, InTASC 2, 3, 7)
2. Understand strategies of orientating new team members to the school and department (ELCC 1.3, ISLLC 1, TLEC 1, 3, InTASC 3, 7)
3. Develop skills in coaching and mentoring teachers and staff (ELCC 1.3, 3.2, ISLLC 1, 3, TLEC 1, 3, InTASC 2, 3, 7)
4. Describe how EEOC laws and regulations impact selecting, coaching, and mentoring employees (ELCC 1.2, 3.2, 5.1, ISLLC 1, 3, 5, TLEC 1, 3, InTASC 3, 7)

INTERVIEWING AND SELECTING APPLICANTS

Undoubtedly, most teacher leaders will be involved in the new employee hiring process. Selecting the right candidate for an open position is not only critical for the team, but also for student learning. The process requires a number of activities such as planning, interviewing, screening, selecting, conducting reference checks, and orientating new employees to the organization.

Much of the work for the interviewing and selection process is done by the human resources department or administration. However, teacher leaders are often involved and will probably participate in the interviewing process. The overall objective is to hire the best candidate for a position and to obtain employment longevity. The process fails when the wrong candidate is hired for a position, which can be a waste of resources and possibly harmful for the school district.

As part of the pre-interviewing process teacher leaders are often involved in applicant screening and candidate selection for an interview. Most applicants submit an application using a state online or district-specific website. Typical information consists of credential files, biographical data, education, licenses and endorsements, student teaching, and past work experience. All information submitted by an applicant should be carefully reviewed and verified prior to selecting candidates for an interview.

Some websites may also include cover letters, references, copies of transcripts, and recommendation letters. These documents and information can generally be scanned into the computer system. A complete application file with all required documents is often required prior to selecting an applicant for an interview. Based upon a review and verification of the applicants' files, candidates are then selected and invited for an interview.

Prior to scheduling the interview session the teacher leader needs to become familiar with all the pre-employment laws that impact interviewing and hiring a candidate. The teacher leader needs to understand permissible and non-permissible questions that can be asked during the interview. For example, it is generally unacceptable to ask a person's age, date of graduation from a college, or on the employment application. These types of questions may violate federal and state laws since they may reveal a person's age and constitute age discrimination.

Questions regarding if an applicant has been arrested are generally unacceptable. Some legal experts feel that there have been a disproportionate number of arrests by minorities in the United States. Therefore, if a school district were to use the number of arrests versus the number of convictions they could be inadvertently discriminating against minority applicants which may violate the Civil Rights Act. However, questions regarding if an applicant has been convicted of a crime are generally appropriate, especially when the nature of the business involves students.

The school board and administrators have a responsibility to keep the students safe and free from potential criminal acts. Generally speaking, felony convictions involving sex, drugs, and physical violence would disqualify an applicant from employment. Keep in mind, that a teacher probably would also not be able to obtain a state teaching license if convicted of these types of crimes. Always consult legal counsel and human resources for guidance on this area.

In preparing for the interview, it is generally advisable for the teacher leader to write out the questions in advance and agree upon all the questions with the screening committee. This information should also be documented and filed should there be an audit by a human rights agency or a claim of discrimination. For example, asking a person's maiden name on an application may reveal a person's ethnicity or race and is generally not acceptable, nor is it generally needed for making a decision whether or not an applicant can perform the essential functions of the job.

Asking questions to applicants about their birthplace, parents, spouse, and other relatives are probably unacceptable since it may reveal a person's national origin. In the United States, an applicant usually does not need to be a U.S. citizen to be employed. Rather, this person simply needs to be legally authorized to work in the country.

It is necessary to obtain verification documents that a person is eligible to work in the country but only after an offer of employment has been extended. Questions such as "Can you produce naturalization papers prior to employment?" or "Were you born in the United States?" are generally unacceptable. It is generally best to ask questions that relate to the requirements and essential elements of the job.

An area that is less clear-cut involves hiring a bilingual or English as a second language (ESL) teacher. The school board may desire to hire a teacher who has a strong cultural appreciation for Hispanic origin and desire to hire a native fluent Spanish-speaking applicant from a Spanish country. It is generally unacceptable to have a requirement that the person be born in a Spanish country or his or her native language is Spanish. The essential question is "Can the applicant do the essential functions of the job?" and it probably doesn't matter the applicant's birthplace.

Questions regarding marital status and gender are not appropriate unless relevant to the job. If an organization is hiring a director of a Jewish women's organization, then it may be appropriate to seek a female who is Jewish. On the other hand, it is generally inappropriate to ask questions to an applicant about sex, marital status, number and ages of children or dependents, obligations for childcare, pregnancy, or child-bearing or birth control, which are generally irrelevant to performing the essential functions of the job.

Another area that has been somewhat controversial in school districts involves an applicant's race, color, and ethnicity. Generally using these factors as a basis for hiring decisions is illegal but may be appropriate in special situations in meeting the affirmative action and diversity requirements or when an organization has established a *bona fide occupational qualification* (BFOQ).

A BFOQ is when an organization establishes a position that is contrary to a federal law because of the nature of the business or core principle of the institution. For example, a BFOQ might be when there is a situation where a religious institution needs to hire a person of a specific religion to satisfy the job requirements. The teacher leader should always follow the direction of the school administration, human resources department, or local counsel on these matters.

Another controversial area in hiring involves applicants with disabilities. The *Americans with Disabilities Act* of 1990 (ADA) prohibits employment discrimination against people with physical or mental disabilities who can perform the essential functions of the job with or without reasonable accommodations. Therefore, during an interview it is generally unacceptable to ask the applicant questions regarding his or her general medical condition, state of health, or other physical or mental disabilities. These questions may reveal medical information that could be used to discriminate against the applicant.

A common question that can be asked by interviewers is "Can you perform the essential functions of the job you are applying for with or without reasonable accommodation?" This question gets to the heart of whether an applicant can perform the basic job which should be the fundamental objective of the interview. Determining the definition of reasonable accommodation can be unclear. Various legal experts have tried to define this term by using past case law.

Once the teacher leader and the search committee have been well trained in pre-employment laws, they need to prepare for conducting the interview. During the preparation phase, the screening committee members should understand as much as they can about the school district. Applicants will undoubtedly have questions about the school district which will need to be answered.

Some of these questions may relate to the union contract, human resource manual, benefits, community and business affiliation, housing availability, and so on. It is often good to prepare a copy of the department organizational chart so that applicants can develop a clear understanding of the people and functions within the department.

During the actual interview session the teacher leader might start out with an icebreaker to make the applicant feel comfortable and to humanize the session. Questions about the traffic or weather are fairly innocuous and can be good ice breakers. The first formal questions are called *data check questions*, which are questions that confirm the applicant's name, the position being applied for and start date. It is not unusual during an interview to find that the wrong applicant is applying for the wrong job at the wrong time and starting out with a data check can help resolve these issues and prevent wasted time and further embarrassment to all parties.

Many candidates may prepare and bring a *personal portfolio*. The items in the portfolio may consist of the candidate's philosophy of education, awards, samples of work, letters of recommendation, transcripts, professional involvement and activities, leadership and community service, professional development activities, skills, and achievements. The portfolio can be a good tool for interviewing committee to get to know the candidate by browsing through the information prior to starting the formal interview questions.

Once the interview session begins it is appropriate to start by introducing all the members of the committee, and providing an overview of the school district. The interviewers then generally begin asking the applicant the formally prepared questions. Some typical interview questions include the following:

1. Describe your teaching style.
2. Describe your teaching philosophy.
3. List examples of professional skill development you have taken in the past five years.
4. Give us an example of how you have handled a difficult student disciplinary problem.
5. What are your greatest strengths?
6. What are your greatest weaknesses?
7. Describe your favorite teaching theories in education.

When preparing questions for the interview some typical areas include instruction, curriculum, discipline, education, experience, interpersonal skills, and teaching style. Questions should be designed that allow the screening committee to obtain information on how well the applicant can perform the essential functions of the job. During the interview session the members should pay close attention to the answers, document responses, and employ effective listening skills.

Some examples of poor listening behaviors include over-reacting to the candidate's responses, lacking eye contact, taking excessive notes that can distract the candidate, and prejudging the person. Also, the teacher leader should acknowledge the candidate's comments and ensure understanding and extend appreciation to the candidate's for participating in the interview.

A part of the interview session should allow the candidate to ask questions about the job and school district. Also, it is often beneficial to provide a tour of the facilities and to promote the school district and community. This helps sell the school and establish good public relations even if the candidate does not take the job.

Many interviewing committees require the candidate to present a demonstration teaching lesson or often called a *mini-teaching presentation*. This allows a realistic opportunity for the interviewing committee to assess the actual teaching performance of the candidate. The format of the mini-teaching presentation often consists of four stages: *preparing, opening, delivering,* and *closing.*

In the *preparing* stage the candidate should present a copy of the lesson plan. This allows the committee to examine how well the candidate has incorporated appropriate pedagogical and instructional components. For example, the lesson plan might consist of behavioral objectives, taxonomy of objectives, domains of learning, instructional techniques, and teaching strategies.

For example, some teaching strategies might consist of problem-based learning, bell ringers, learning styles, multiple intelligence, curriculum compacting, simulation, case studies, behavioral skills modeling, and cooperative and collaborative learning. Teacher leaders need to carefully assess the level of quality and soundness of the lesson plan. If the lesson plan lacks these basic components then this should be a red flag of concern for the committee.

There are many reasons why mini-teaching presentations can fail. Some of these include the following:

1. Poorly designed lesson plan.
2. Failure to set up the audio visual equipment or technology.
3. Not speaking clearly and stating distracting phrases.
4. Failure to answer questions correctly.
5. Failure to engage the participants.
6. Using the wrong teaching strategy for a lesson objective.
7. Poor closing or evaluation component in the closing.

All the interview committee members should evaluate the mini-teaching presentation using an appropriate instructional evaluation form. Typically these forms are available at the school district office administration or research and professional development department.

When preparing for the mini-presentation, the committee should ask the candidate what resources and equipment are needed for the session. They should also make sure that everything is available and ready for the candidate. In some cases the school technician should be available during the start of the session in case technical support is needed. For example, some of the equipment the technician might test include the computer, PowerPoint software program, projector, video, and station controls to be assured that everything is working. The technician may also need to explain the operation of the equipment to the candidate.

Once the candidate begins the presentation, the committee members should assess the *opening.* Without a doubt the opening can be the most difficult part of the session. Some of the elements to assess include how well the candidate states the objectives, engages the participants, explains the purpose of the lesson, includes an attention getter, maintains eye contact, establishes a receptive learning environment, and communicates in a clear and concise manner.

Another skill that is needed by candidates is the ability to make effective *transitions*. A transition is the ability for the candidate to smoothly move from one topic to another in a logical manner that is easily followed by the participants. Candidates who are nervous may forget some of these points. Some techniques for effective transitions include these:

- Momentarily pausing before moving to the next slide or topic.
- Allowing for questions and answers (in accordance with the learning objectives established during the opening).
- Summarizing the information before introducing the next segment.
- Explaining how one topic relates to another.
- Telling the participants of the next topic.

The *delivering* stage comprises the main body of the mini-teaching presentation. In this stage the candidate undoubtedly will be using some combination of PowerPoint slides, Prezi, handouts, smart board, lecture, or discussion formats. The committee members should assess how well the candidate presents the content, flow of information, answers questions, projects and modulates his or her voice, speaks enthusiastically, gives good eye contact, and uses good principles of learning. In addition, they should assess how well the candidate uses nonverbal and listening techniques and maintains the interest of the participants.

The last part of the mini-teaching presentation is the *closing*. A good closing should have a smooth ending that brings the participants attention to the main purpose and objective of the lesson. The closing should also include some type of assessment. The interview committee should evaluate how well the candidate incorporates various assessment techniques into the closing. Some typical examples include a quiz, observation, questions and answers, role play, demonstration, and portfolio essay.

Once the mini-teaching presentation has ended the interview comes to the last stage. Generally, the committee chair or human resource director asks the candidate permission to obtain reference checks, receives a signature from the candidate for conducting the background check, permission to take a drug test or medical examination. The committee chair should then explain the next steps and thank the candidate for participating in the interview.

Committee members should also refrain from giving candidates an impression that they will receive a job offer. It is often customary to inform the candidate that once all candidates have been interviewed, and a decision has been made, and they will be notified. Candidates are generally notified in writing of the decision, and candidates who are being given an offer for employment are often called on the telephone.

After the interview session has concluded, more work is required in the *postsession phase*. This phase is critical for the teacher leader and screening committee members to thoroughly evaluate the applicant and make decisions for the next steps. Figure 4.1 provides a sample of a typical interview evaluation form.

Name of Applicant:			Interview Date:		
Position:			Lead Interviewer:		
Please complete the questions below after interviewing the applicant.					
	Unable to evaluate	Below average	Average	Above average	Excellent
EDUCATION (general background and knowledge)	0	1	2	3	4
TEACHING EXPERIENCE (curriculum and instruction)	0	1	2	3	4
INTERPERSONAL SKILLS (ability to relate to people)	0	1	2	3	4
COMMUNICATION SKILLS (verbal, non-verbal and written skills)	0	1	2	3	4
TECHNOLOGY SKILLS (proficiency in using technology)	0	1	2	3	4
				TOTAL SCORE	_____
Rating Recommendation (circle one)	Hire	Consider		Do not hire	
Comments					
Interview Team:					
1.					
2.					
3.					

Figure 4.1.   Example of Interview Evaluation Form

There are many types of evaluation forms that can be used to assess an applicant after an interview. Every school district should develop a form that is best for the organization and is legally compliant. It is generally advisable to meet as soon as possible after an interview to capture everyone's impressions and review comments.

Some typical categories to evaluate include education knowledge, teaching experience, interpersonal and communications, and technology skills. The decision whether to extend an offer to a candidate can also be discussed. Also, comments justifying a member's rating decision should be documented. When completed, all interview evaluation forms should be collected, filed and kept for future use should there be an audit or discrimination claim.

ORIENTATING, COACHING, AND MENTORING EMPLOYEES

Once a candidate has been employed, the next step is to conduct a proper new employee orientation program (Haggarty, 2011). This is especially important for new teachers and staff members entering the education environment for the first time. A good orientation program can often increase the chances of the new teacher or staff member being successful.

An orientation program should provide an opportunity to clarify job responsibilities and expectations, understand the history of the school district, meet fellow teachers and staff members, understand policies and procedures, and become comfortable with the new work environment. Figure 4.2 lists some of the typical employee orientation information covered for new employees.

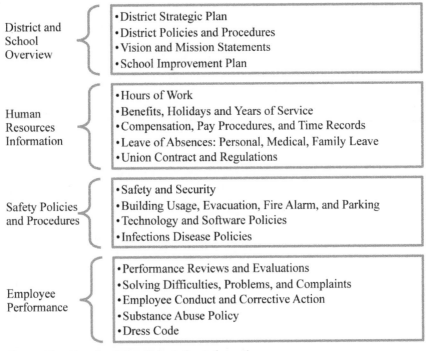

District and School Overview
- District Strategic Plan
- District Policies and Procedures
- Vision and Mission Statements
- School Improvement Plan

Human Resources Information
- Hours of Work
- Benefits, Holidays and Years of Service
- Compensation, Pay Procedures, and Time Records
- Leave of Absences: Personal, Medical, Family Leave
- Union Contract and Regulations

Safety Policies and Procedures
- Safety and Security
- Building Usage, Evacuation, Fire Alarm, and Parking
- Technology and Software Policies
- Infections Disease Policies

Employee Performance
- Performance Reviews and Evaluations
- Solving Difficulties, Problems, and Complaints
- Employee Conduct and Corrective Action
- Substance Abuse Policy
- Dress Code

Figure 4.2. New Employee Orientation Information

Research has shown that up to one-third of new teachers leave a school district within three years (National Center for Educational Statistics, 2012). There are several reasons for teacher attrition such as: high expectations by administrators, long working hours, preparing lesson plans, grading, and dealing with student and parent problems. Therefore, providing meaningful new teacher orientation and mentoring programs can help support new teachers and reduce attrition.

Once the new orientation program has been completed, one of the most effective strategies that can support a new teacher is a mentoring program (Hanson, 2010). Generally speaking, all teachers can benefit from good coaching and mentoring. Teacher leaders serve a valuable role in this process. Mentoring can help teachers when faced with issues in dealing with disruptive students, personal problems that impact teaching, administrative requirements, and clarifying the responsibilities of the position.

All teacher leader mentors should be well trained in how to be an effective coach. Topics might include understanding instruction and curriculum, managing student discipline, understanding the school district operations, and district policies and procedures. In addition to these professional qualities, an effective mentor needs effective coaching skills which include being personal, sensitive, understanding, establishing rapport, and giving constructive feedback. Mentors should also be evaluated by administrators to ensure their performance is acceptable.

Figure 4.3 lists typical information for a teacher mentoring program. When working with a new teacher the teacher leader mentor should begin by establishing rapport. He or she should cover the basics teaching responsibilities, lesson plan preparation, strategies in beginning a class, completing student absentee records, and classroom management. Other items might include dealing with student academic problems, responding to a fire or disaster drill, and dealing with parent issues.

One of the most important topics to cover with all teachers is time management and multitasking skills. Some of the common timewasters for a teacher include telephone interruptions, inadequate planning, over socializing, meetings, procrastinating, dealing with confused responsibilities or expectations, poor communications, and personal disorganization.

A good mentor should be able to coach teachers on these time wasters and offer strategies for overcoming them which might include listing goals for each day, preparing work in advance, making a daily to-do list, eliminating unproductive activities, and setting deadlines for accomplishing work tasks. One-on-one coaching can be valuable in assisting the teacher in improving time management and performance.

The teacher leader mentor should make regular, *formative observations* of teachers' instruction and provide timely feedback. Formative feedback is an on-going review designed to give informal assessment without the

School facilities and equipment

• Orientation and location of media equipment, technology, supplies, special services, parking, etc.

School procedures

• Hours of work, attendance, policies, dress code, crisis management, testing policies, student emergencies, etc.

Resource access

• Use of discretionary funds, shared equipment and materials, textbooks, supplemental materials, classroom teaching supplies, requisitions, etc.

Curriculum and instruction

• Lesson plan procedures and expectations, subject matter experts, grading procedures, school calendar and schedule, curriculum mapping, district office expectations, and location of guide manuals.

Student discipline management

• Student discipline procedures and expectations, how to handle disciplinary offenses, initiating a parent conference, the referral process, etc.

Figure 4.3. Examples of Information in a Mentor Program

formal supervisory evaluation, which becomes part of the new teacher's performance record.

The basic steps for conducting a formative teacher observation include preconference, observation, analysis, and postconference feedback. During the preconference discussion the mentor schedules the time and place for observation in collaboration with the teacher. Teacher leaders should utilize the district's *framework for teaching* such as the Danielson model for observing teachers throughout the entire observation process (Danielson, 2007).

A *framework for teaching* is a research-based instructional guideline that links teaching responsibilities and activities together that can be measured. For example, the Danielson model encompasses four domains: planning and preparation, classroom environment, instruction, and professional responsibilities (Danielson, 2007).

When assessing teachers, based upon a framework for teaching, a rubric should always be used. The rubric describes various levels of performance such as unsatisfactory, needs improvement, meets performance, and exceeds performance. There are several types of rubrics and evaluation scales and teacher leaders should use them consistently within the district.

During the observation the teacher leader should record and evaluate teachers on all aspects of teaching and classroom management. Afterward a careful analysis and review of the information should be completed in preparation for the postconference meeting. During this meeting the teacher leader mentor should give constructive feedback to the teacher.

At times, the teacher leader may need to provide *on-the-job training* for a teacher or staff member. For example, the teacher leader may need to explain how to use a specific school software program, learning resource, instructional technology, complete a curriculum form, or operate equipment. There are several steps in conducing on-the-job training which are described in figure 4.4.

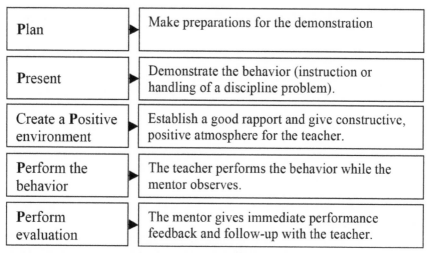

Plan	Make preparations for the demonstration
Present	Demonstrate the behavior (instruction or handling of a discipline problem).
Create a Positive environment	Establish a good rapport and give constructive, positive atmosphere for the teacher.
Perform the behavior	The teacher performs the behavior while the mentor observes.
Perform evaluation	The mentor gives immediate performance feedback and follow-up with the teacher.

Figure 4.4.   The Five Steps to On-The-Job Mentor Training

The teacher leader mentor should regularly provide casual feedback by asking questions such as "Describe things that are going well for you," "Describe some areas that you would like to improve," "What things can I do as a teacher leader to better assist you?" The feedback given to teachers and staff members, in addition to being a formative process, can also be summative.

Summative feedback is conducted generally by the teacher evaluator or administrator and is used as a formal and official record of performance. For example, a formal and documented performance evaluation is generally considered to be a summative process. Many states require that the teacher leader complete and pass state training to be qualified to give summative performance evaluations. Details on performance evaluations are given in chapter six.

Providing *effective coaching* for all teachers, whether new or experienced, is a major responsibility of teacher leaders. All teacher leaders should be well trained in providing coaching for teachers and staff. Examples of coaching topics include instruction and curriculum, classroom management, handling discipline, using instructional technology, and administrative requirements. Figure 4.5 lists steps in conducting a coaching session.

Step 1	Describe the performance.
Step 2	State expectations or standards.
Step 3	Ask teacher to reflect on performance.
Step 4	Listen, empathize and paraphrase.
Step 5	Identify problem and root cause.
Step 6	Ask for solutions to resolve problem.
Step 7	Discuss and agree upon actions.
Step 8	Thank the teacher and build his or her confidence.

Figure 4.5. Steps in Conducting a Formative Employee Coaching Session

During the first step of the formative coaching session the teacher leader should *describe the performance* of the new teacher. During this stage the teacher leader begins by humanizing the setting, and being objective and direct in describing performance that needs to be improved. For example, issues might include the need for improved instruction, handling of a student disciplinary case, or improving lesson plans.

Step two requires the teacher leader to describe the *desired expectation* or standard. For example, the teacher leader may state that lesson plans need to be error free, well organized, and contain all components outlined in the school policy manual. Examples may be given to the teacher to show the desired expectation.

Step three involves the teacher *reflecting upon his or her performance* and identifying positive behaviors and areas in need of improvement. This reflection can be a valuable method to help a teacher examine his or her performance without the teacher leader directly stating the problem. For example, the teacher may conclude that he or she is having difficulty handling student misbehavior and needs to better administer the school district policies.

An important step in the coaching session is for the teacher leader to *sincerely listen, paraphrase* and *empathize* with his or her feelings, and paraphrase the teacher's comments (step four). The use of paraphrasing helps to verify what the teacher stated and confirm mutual understanding. Typical statements might be "I can understand how you feel in a situation like this," "I can see how someone would have these feelings in a situation like this," or "I was once a new teacher as well and understand."

Paraphrasing can also help to show that the teacher leader is demonstrating active listening and helps in personalizing the conversation and developing an atmosphere of respect. In addition paraphrasing ensures understanding of the message being communicated and this technique can be helpful for both the teacher leader and teacher.

Step five involves the teacher *identifying the root cause* of the performance problem. This step is similar to step three but goes into greater detail. For example, if a teacher is experiencing difficulty in handling disciplinary problems the potential root causes might include: distractions from outside influences, health issues, a poor attitude, need for additional training or a dysfunctional school environment. It is important for the teacher leader to reinforce the teacher's responsibility for improvement and to provide encouragement for improvement.

The sixth step entails *asking the teacher for solutions* for the performance issue. In this way the teacher is more likely to accept the solution. It also allows the new teacher to take responsibility for his or her own behavior. For example, the teacher may need to include more engaging instructional activities or learn to control to his or her emotions when dealing with student misbehavior.

In step seven the teacher leader and teacher should *discuss and agree upon an action plan* for resolving the performance issue. There may be some negotiation so they can collaboratively resolve the issue. The teacher should propose a solution that is acceptable to the teacher leader since he or she will be more apt to accept the solution rather than it being imposed upon him or her. However, if the teacher's suggestion is unacceptable to the teacher leader mentor further discussion may be necessary and ultimately they will need to mutually arrive to an effective action.

The last step, step eight, involves the teacher leader *thanking the teacher* for participating in the coaching session and building his or her confidence. Building the confidence of a teacher has reinforcing consequences. It may also be worthwhile to schedule a follow-up session to review progress of the teacher's performance.

Even if a teacher leader has difficulty in supporting a teacher, especially because of very poor performance incidents, the teacher leader needs to continue to maintain a positive working relationship. Otherwise the coach-teacher relationship will be undermined and the teacher may resort to retaliatory actions that become stressful and time consuming.

During the coaching process the teacher leader should also be aware of his or her subtle, nonverbal cues that the teacher may observe that are incongruent with the teacher leader's verbal message. For example, stating something positive to the teacher, but coming across with defensive body language. The teacher leader may also suggest a follow-up session to review the teacher's progress.

When giving constructive feedback, a teacher leader needs to be aware of the typical *defense mechanisms* that are often displayed by teachers (see figure 4.6). Defense mechanisms are those things that human beings do to protect themselves from experiencing bad feelings. People typically desire to avoid feeling bad, and defense mechanisms can help reduce or eliminate these feelings.

Teachers, and all team members, can often feel vulnerable, especially if they experience several setbacks. Consequently, they may resort to

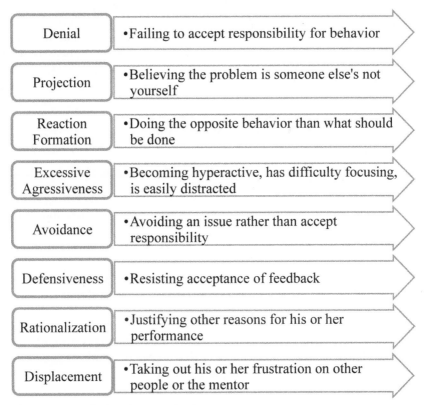

Denial	• Failing to accept responsibility for behavior
Projection	• Believing the problem is someone else's not yourself
Reaction Formation	• Doing the opposite behavior than what should be done
Excessive Agressiveness	• Becoming hyperactive, has difficulty focusing, is easily distracted
Avoidance	• Avoiding an issue rather than accept responsibility
Defensiveness	• Resisting acceptance of feedback
Rationalization	• Justifying other reasons for his or her performance
Displacement	• Taking out his or her frustration on other people or the mentor

Figure 4.6. Typical Defense Mechanisms

defense mechanisms to prevent themselves from feeling bad. Teacher leaders need to pay close attention to the behaviors and comments of teachers and recognize when defense mechanism are being used. Providing coaching can help teachers deal with these defense mechanisms and help ameliorate bad feelings.

UNDERSTANDING EMPLOYMENT LAWS WHEN COACHING

There are a myriad of federal and state laws and executive orders that impact teacher leaders in coaching and mentoring teachers. The administration of these laws is the responsibility of the human resources department and administration. Teacher leaders need to understand these laws, especially if they do coaching and teacher evaluations. They should always consult with the human resources department or administration.

While there are many federal laws impacting education, there are also specific laws unique to individual states and school district policies. While federal laws tend to trump state and local laws, all of these laws must be understood and practiced by teacher leaders and administrators.

State laws and regulations often govern certification and licensing regulations. Local school boards may establish higher standards than state regulations but generally cannot legally establish lower standards. All teacher leaders and administrators must be well informed and seek local counsel in understanding the interrelationship of federal, state, and local school board laws and regulations.

For example, as an outgrowth of the civil rights movement of the 1960s, the Equal Employment Opportunity Commission (EEOC) was established by *Title VII of the 1964 Civil Rights Act*. The original act prohibited discrimination on the basis of race, color, religion, national origin, and gender. This law covered many aspects of employment including hiring, supervising, compensating, coaching, mentoring, promoting, and terminating employees.

While the *Civil Rights Act* primarily covered all employers in public and private institutions with fifteen or more employees, the act provided the guidelines for bringing litigation against institutions that practiced discriminatory acts. The penalties associated with *Civil Rights Act* violations can be severe.

The various civil rights laws allow individuals who have been discriminated against to seek compensatory and punitive damages for both willful and intentional discrimination acts. Compensatory damages generally involve harm to an employee for pain and emotional suffering. Punitive damages can be assessed against an employer which serves as punishment and a deterrent for others. There are some limitations for judgment awards depending upon the size of an organization.

In addition to the EEOC, violations of discrimination are also enforced and judgments can be awarded by state human rights commissions. For example, the State of Illinois has a Department of Human Rights Commission, which is responsible for protecting individuals from discriminatory practices. This agency is responsible for providing guidelines for both public and private organizations.

Also, local school district may have policies that supplement federal and state laws. These are only some of the basics of the EEOC and related laws that impact teacher leaders when coaching teachers and staff. Keeping abreast of the bulletins and compliance information by the human resource department is essential for all teacher leaders.

SUMMARY

The job of the teacher leader in selecting, coaching, and mentoring teachers is a critical one. Teacher leaders need to understand and develop skills in selecting, orientating, mentoring, coaching, listening, communicating, and adhering to federal and state laws. Also, understanding the goals of the organization, anticipating changes in staffing, staying current with laws and local district policies, and working with school administrators and human resources are critical for teacher leaders.

Proper planning allows for all teacher leaders to develop a framework to recruit, select, hire, mentor, and develop future people to meet staffing needs. Also, effective coaching and mentoring can help develop high-performing employees. The role of the teacher leader is an important one in supporting the administration in achieving excellence and student learning.

CASE STUDY

Edison High School—Creating a 90-Day Entry Plan

Edison High School is a magnet school in an urban environment serving about 1,200 students. You are a teacher leader and you were involved in the hiring of three new teachers in your department. The principal has asked you to prepare a written ninety-day entry plan for orientating and mentoring the new teachers.

This entry plan will serve as a model for other teacher leaders and the principal would like to present it to the school board members at the next board meeting. Prepare this ninety-day entry plan including aspects such as orientating, mentoring process, logistics and time table, expectations, legal considerations, staff introductions, meeting schedule, budget, and instruction and curriculum, and so on.

EXERCISES AND DISCUSSION QUESTIONS

1. Describe some of the major legal issues impacting the interviewing and selection process that a teacher leader needs to understand and practice. Also, research and list some laws unique to your state and how they support federal laws.
2. List and explain the laws that protect people on the basis of race, sex, religion, national origin, age and disability and how these laws can be difficult to administer in some school districts.
3. Describe the components of a comprehensive new employee orientation program.
4. Describe effective coaching and mentoring strategies that a teacher leader can use for improving employee performance.

REFERENCES

Danielson, C. (2007). *Enhancing professional practice*. Alexandria, VA: Association for Supervision and Curriculum Development.

Haggarty, L. (2011). Improving the learning of newly qualified teachers in the induction year. *British Educational Research Journal*, 3(6), 935–954.

Hanson, S. (2010). What mentors learn about teaching. *Educational Leadership*, 6(8), 76-80.

National Center for Education Statistics: www.nces.ed.gov/2012.

Tomal, D. (2013). *Managing human resources and collective bargaining*. Lanham, MD: The Rowman & Littlefield Education, Inc.

United States Equal Employment Opportunity Commission: (2011). www.eeoc.gov/laws.

Chapter 5

Leading and Motivating

OBJECTIVES

At the conclusion of this chapter you will be able to:

1. Understand principles and theories of leadership that apply to teacher leaders (ELCC 1.1, 1.3, 1.4, 5.1, ISLLC 1, 5, TLEC 1, 3, InTASC 2, 3, 7)
2. Understand principles and theories of motivation from the perspective of teacher leaders (ELCC 1.3, 1.4, ISLLC 1, TLEC 1, 3, InTASC 2, 3, 7)
3. Apply strategies for leading and motivating employees as a teacher leader (ELCC 1.1, 1.3, 1.4, ISLLC 1, TLEC 1, 3, InTASC 2, 3, 7)
4. Apply strategies for building teamwork and collaboration as a teacher leader (ELCC 1.3, 1.4, 3.2, ISLLC 1, 3, TLEC 1, 3, InTASC 2, 7)

LEADING TEAM MEMBERS

Effective teacher leaders need to understand and practice effective leadership and motivation principles and strategies to maximize employee performance. One important objective of teacher leaders is the ability to understand the vision and strategic goals of the school district and to work with the teachers and staff in accomplishing them. One way to achieve this objective is to develop effective leadership skills and apply these leadership skills directly with team members.

One characteristic of an effective teacher leader is that of *role modeling.* Teacher leaders serve as the role model for employees and are expected to understand and practice good behaviors that support the values of the organization. Good followers often make good leaders. The ability to effectively inspire team members and to exhibit effective leadership characteristics is critical in modeling these characteristics for employees.

One of the more popular leadership theories that has practical applicability to leading employees was developed by Paul Hersey and Kenneth Blanchard titled *Situational Leadership* (see figure 5.1). This theory builds upon the leadership styles of other people who developed a continuum of leadership behaviors ranging from authoritarian to participatory. This theory can be valuable in helping leaders understand the best styles in leading employees given the situation and people being led.

	Participate (S$_3$)	Sell (S$_2$)
High	High Relationship Low Task	High Task High Relationship
Low	Delegate (S$_4$)	Tell (S$_1$)
	Low Relationship Low Task	High Task Low Relationship

Relationship (High ↕ Low)

| Low ← Task Behavior → High |
| High ← Maturity → Low |

Figure 5.1.   Situational Leadership Model
Source: Paul Hersey and Ken Blanchard, 1977.

To understand this theory, there are several terms that need to be defined. *Task behavior* can be defined as one-way communication (directive behavior) from a teacher leader to an employee. When a teacher leader uses the task behavior, he or she is giving direct instructions to an employee. The task behavior is directive and there is basically no interchange or conversation. In this style, the employee is basically listening to the teacher leader.

The term *relationship behavior* can be described as two-way communication between a teacher leader and employee. The relationship behavior is very supportive, and it is considered to be two-way discussion. This behavior also assumes that there is a high emphasis placed upon both communicating and listening.

The term *maturity* can be described as the degree of an employee's positive attitude, experience, and overall emotional maturity in performing the job. The maturity level ranges from low to moderate to high. If an employee has low maturity, he or she is considered to be immature. A high maturity level would describe an employee as being very mature in his or her attitude and behavior.

In the situational leadership model there are four leadership styles. Style one (S1) is called *telling*. In this style the teacher leader uses a high task and a low relationship behavior. This would be an example where the teacher leader is giving one-way direction to an employee and there is virtually no discussion. For instance, a teacher leader could use this style when explaining the job requirements to a new administrative assistant on his or her first day of work.

The second style is called *selling* (S2). This style uses high task and high relationship behaviors. In this style the teacher leader is engaging in directive conversation with an employee. This style considers that the maturity level of the employee is in between low and moderate. For example, this style can be useful when needing to persuade an employee to accept new policies of an organization.

The next leadership style is called *participating* (S3). In this style, the teacher leader uses high relationship and low task behaviors. This leadership style assumes that the maturity level of the employee is in between moderate to high. In this situation the teacher leader would engage in two-way conversation with the employee.

The last leadership style is called *delegating* (S4). This style uses low relationship and low task behaviors. It also assumes the maturity level of the employee is high. This is a typical situation when a seasoned teacher knows the job very well. The teacher leader simply needs to delegate the work to the teacher and let him or her teach the class. This style requires little interaction and communications between the teacher leader and teacher.

Let's examine an example of how a teacher leader could use the situational leadership theory in leading an employee. If a teacher leader has a new teacher assigned to a classroom, it can be assumed that the teacher will most likely have a low maturity given that he or she does not understand the expectations of the job nor is familiar with the department. In this situation, the teacher leader may begin using the style of *telling*.

The *telling style* would assume that the teacher knows virtually nothing about the classroom assignment and, therefore, the teacher leader would need to exhibit high task and low relationship behaviors. The teacher leader would begin by explaining the assignment and expectations while the employee listens. There would be no need for two-way discussion given that the teacher initially is only receiving information.

As the teacher begins to mature and starts to understand the expectations there becomes a need for both high task and high relationship behavior by the teacher leader. In this situation the teacher would use the style of *selling*. This style assumes that there is two-way conversation with the teacher, but is still directive. For example, the teacher might begin asking questions and participate in conversation with the teacher leader, even though the teacher leader would still need to be somewhat directive.

As the new teacher continues to mature and develops more of a moderate to high maturity level, the teacher leader would then use the style of *participating*. The *participating* style assumes that there is a need for high relationship and low task behaviors. In this situation, the teacher leader needs to continue two-way conversations and there is little need for the teacher leader to be very directive.

As the teacher continues to mature and develops a high maturity level the teacher leader would then use the style of *delegating*. In this situation, there is a need for low relationship and low task behaviors. When the teacher has a high maturity level, the teacher leader no longer needs to engage in lengthy two-way discussion but rather delegates the job but is available for discussion.

An example of a new teacher and his or her maturity development provides an effective situation for a teacher leader to utilize all four styles of situational leadership in an appropriate manner. While variations may occur in the teacher's maturity level, the teacher leader constantly should beware of assessing this maturity level and adapt his or her style appropriately.

The *situational leadership* model takes in consideration three major aspects—the style of the leader, the employee(s) being lead, and the situation. For example, the situational leadership model does not indicate that there is only one style, rather the models suggest that the teacher leader should use the appropriate style given the situation and maturity level of the employees.

Another example might be when a teacher leader observes a staff member engaging in disruptive behavior. The teacher leader most likely would to use the leadership style of *telling*. In this case the teacher leader would be very directive in asking the staff member to correct the behavior. This style would be appropriate given the situation and behavior of the employee.

The *telling* style is often appropriate when a teacher leader needs quick directive change in behavior. Another example where the telling style may be appropriate is in the case of an emergency. If there is a fire drill and directive instructions need to be given to all employees, the teacher leader would use the telling style. In this situation, there is no need for discussion but rather the teacher leader needs to act decisively in ensuring the safety of all employees.

The *selling* leadership style is one that a teacher leader may find very useful when needing to convince an employee to improve his or her performance. When an employee's performance needs to improve, using the telling style may create resentment and the selling style may be best to establish a professional two-way discussion but, at the same time, be firm and directive.

The *participating* leadership style can be effective when dealing with an employee who has a moderate to high maturity level. For example, if a teacher leader has an employee who is having difficulty solving a problem the two-way conversation may be the best leadership style. In this situation, the staff member is more apt to accept constructive feedback and improve.

The *delegating* leadership style can be very effective when dealing with an employee who has a high maturity level. For example, if the employee is working on a project and is fully capable of completing it, then the teacher leader should back off and give the person member the necessary authority and empowerment. The delegating style can be very effective in allowing high maturity employees to make decisions without need for much interaction.

The main principle of the situational leadership theory is that the teacher leader needs to use the most effective style given the situation and the people being led. For example, a teacher leader may have an employee who has a high maturity level, but is starting to slip. In this case, if the employee's maturity is lower the teacher leader may need to use the *participating* or *telling* style to correct the behavior.

A unique aspect of applying the situational leadership theory is its dynamic aspect. The teacher leader may find himself or herself simultaneously using the telling, selling, participating, and delegating styles on a frequent basis. The teacher leader may be using one-way directive (telling) behavior with an employee and then switch to a participating style with another. The teacher leader's ability to switch the styles is a key in successfully applying this theory.

One danger for a teacher leader in using this style is in becoming dependent on using one style too frequently. A teacher leader may be viewed as being too autocratic if consistently using the *telling* style. This style most likely will not be effective in dealing with all employees all the time. Likewise, if the supervisor only used the *delegating* style this could be viewed as abdication.

One of the landmark theories in developing positive leadership was proposed by Douglas McGregor. He suggested that leaders largely fall

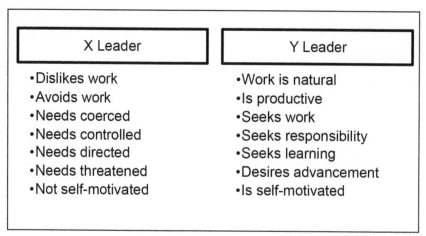

Figure 5.2.   Theory X and Y
Source: adapted from Douglas McGregor, *The Human Side of Enterprise*, NY, McGraw-Hill 1960.

into one of two styles—*Theory X* or *Theory Y* (see figure 5.2). He believed that leaders tend to make assumptions about employees and their attitude toward work.

McGregor felt that a Theory X leader assumes that people are lazy, irresponsible, and need to be coerced, controlled, and directed in order for them to perform work. He felt that Theory X leaders view their workers as people who inherently dislike work and have little ambition.

The Theory Y leader, on the other hand, believes people are creative, self-directed, desire to work, responsible, resourceful, and seeks advancement. Simply stated, McGregor felt that the Theory X leader is negative and disrespects workers, and that the Theory Y leader is positive and respectful toward workers.

McGregor's theory has wide implications for leading employees. For example, if a teacher leader assumes the Theory X assumption, then the teacher leader will most likely be very directive and threatening to employees. The teacher leader may develop a sarcastic attitude. The employee will, in turn, behave and perform accordingly.

In other words, if you don't expect much you don't get much. If people are treated as if they are lazy and irresponsible, then they often perform to the leaders' expectations. This style can have a conditioning effect on employees and be harmful to the entire organization. An entire negative organizational culture can be created.

While some teacher leaders may not vividly exhibit Theory X behavior, people can often recognize the blatant and subtle cues from the person. If a teacher leader has Theory X tendencies subtle signs could be seen through their gestures. For example, the teacher leader may have less eye contact with people, exhibit a frown, or use a negative tone of voice.

Moreover, the subtle use of a teacher leader's body language can be revealing. For example, if the teacher leader tends to point his or her finger and talk in a condescending manner toward employees, these cues become very obvious and reveal the teacher leader's true assumptions. Teacher leaders need to be always aware of the body language that they are projecting when coaching and leading employees

The Theory Y teacher leader is one who exhibits a positive attitude toward employees. This teacher leader promotes a healthy atmosphere and motivates people to perform their best. The teacher leader's assumption is to expect the best of the people and they, in turn, will often perform to their expectations.

The most important significance of McGregor's theory is that the assumptions that teacher leaders, as leaders, have toward their employees can create a *self-fulfilling prophecy.* The notion of the self-fulfilling prophecy is that a belief in an event or expectation can actually cause it to happen. Therefore, if teacher leaders don't expect much from their employees they will not get much.

On the other hand, if teacher leaders place high expectations on people, then they will often perform to their high expectations. The concept of *self-fulfilling prophecy* can be seen in many aspects of life. In the sports arena, the concept of the self-fulfilling prophecy is widely used. If a coach places high expectations on his or her players, the players will often perform to those expectations. This is similar to the coaching of teacher leaders and employees.

For example, if a coach removes a player from the game at a critical moment because he or she does not believe the player can succeed and replaces the player with another player, these expectations can have reinforcing consequences. The player who is removed often will continue to perform less while the player who the coach has confidence in often improves his or her performance.

One leadership model designed specifically for teacher leaders is called the Teacher Leader Capability Model (see figure 5.3). This leadership model illustrates four types (quadrants) of teacher leaders depending upon the degree of the teacher leaders' competence and confidence: *obnoxious teacher leader, incapable teacher leader, timid teacher leader*, and the *capable teacher leader* (Tomal, 2007).

In order to understand the model, three terms need to be defined: *competence, confidence*, and *self-management*. *Competence* refers to the teacher leader's ability to effectively lead and motivate people. High competence indicates that the teacher leader has the ability to understand leadership

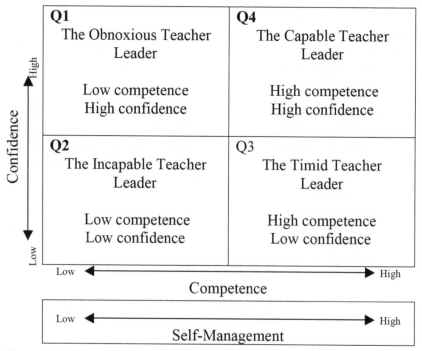

Figure 5.3. Teacher Leader Capability Model

and motivation strategies and how to effectively use these strategies to effectively lead and motivate people.

The second term, teacher leader *confidence* indicates a teacher leader's feelings of adequacy and self-reliance in leading and coaching people. A teacher leader with high confidence has strong spirit, tenacity, courage, and resolution with his or her ability as a leader. A teacher leader who has low confidence would be apprehensive, experience feelings of self-doubt, and uncertainty when leading and motivating people.

The third term in understanding the model is *self-management*. Self-management refers to the teacher leader's degree of experience, knowledge, and resourcefulness as a leader. Self-management indicates how skillful the teacher leader is in having a good self-concept and belief in his or her abilities as a leader. Self-management goes beyond only being competent or confident and suggests the quality of experience and fortitude in actually applying both confidence and competence in leadership.

In applying the teacher leadership capability model to leading and coaching school employees, if a teacher leader has low self-management but also low competence and a high confidence could be referred to as the *obnoxious teacher leader* (Q1). This teacher leader, while having high confidence in leading and motivating people, does not have the competence and, therefore, will demotivate people. This typical teacher leader is one who is undoubtedly assertive in attempting to lead people but is ineffective given the lack of knowledge and skills.

The second type of teacher leader is the *incapable teacher leader* (Q2). This teacher leader would have low self-management, and low competence and confidence. The teacher leader would have the qualities of not being confident or competent in his or her ability to lead and motivate people. This teacher leader would not have an understanding of leadership and motivational factors and would be ineffective in leading people.

The third type of leader is called the *timid teacher leader* (Q3). This is a teacher leader who may have high competence but lacks confidence in effectively leading and motivating people. While this teacher leader may have high self-management in terms of understanding effective strategies for leading and motivating people, the leader is ineffective given his or her lack of confidence.

The fourth type of leader is the *capable teacher leader* (Q4). This leader incorporates a high self-management (understands leadership and motivation strategies) and has both high competence and high confidence. This is an effective teacher leader who is able to understand both intrinsic and extrinsic motivators and how to effectively apply them in motivating people.

The effectiveness of applying this model rests with the understanding that teacher leaders need high self-management to be effective in leading people. Being a *capable teacher leader* goes well beyond just the understanding of leadership and motivational strategies, but also requires the need for high confidence in order to be an effective leader.

For example, if a teacher leader has a group of teachers who are apathetic and consistently demonstrate poor performance, then the possibility of the leader having both low confidence and competence may exist. This teacher leader, in essence, may be the *incapable teacher leader* and needs to develop high self-management abilities in understanding leadership and motivational strategies, and the competence in applying these strategies.

On the other hand, a teacher leader who may be very motivated and self-assured to apply strategies, but lacks the actual competence, would still have low self-management because of his or her inability to understand the leadership motivation strategies. In this case, the appropriate style would be used effectively in this situation.

However, the teacher leader who can be described as the *timid teacher leader* would be one who has a group of employees who may also have performance problems and high motivation. This *timid teacher leader* may be very effective in writing the rules for performance standards but may have difficulty in actually applying the strategies given his or her low confidence.

The *capable teacher leader* most likely would have a group of employees who are motivated and have good performance due to his or her ability to communicate rules and procedures of good performance. He or she also has the skills to apply these strategies to the work setting. The use of this model can be valuable in not only leading and coaching employees, but motivating them as well (Tomal, 2007).

MOTIVATING TEAM MEMBERS

"You can lead a horse to water but you can't make him drink" is a familiar saying that many leaders can relate to. Motivation is a difficult term to define. Essentially it is the willingness of a person to partake in an endeavor in order to satisfy a person's need. Human beings have an innate desire to satisfy basic physiological and psychological needs.

The ability to influence employees to be motivated to have a desire to achieve a goal is an overall objective of teacher leaders. While there are many different educational theories regarding motivation, most of them have a common underlying theme regarding the human needs of people. Developing and understanding human needs can be very valuable in motivating employees (Nohia, Groysberg, and Lee, 2010).

Abraham Maslow (1943) articulated one of the first theories on human needs by classifying them into five different levels. The lower order needs (first two levels) consist of basic physiological needs including safety and security. The higher order needs (upper three levels) consist of belonging and social needs, esteem and status needs, and self-actualization and fulfillment (see figure 5.4).

Maslow's hierarchy is highly relevant to motivating employees today. People seek different amounts of specific needs than others. Some individuals simply have a higher need for security than other people. For example, many people feel insecure when living paycheck to paycheck. Some people are greatly stressed by not having any savings account while others feel that as long as they are not in debt everything is fine. Likewise, employees may have different need levels. Some employees simply may need more attention than others.

Therefore, employees' desires to fill their human needs in the workplace involve a multiplicity of factors such as peer group identification, sense of duty, collaboration, desire for a promotion, attitude toward the school board, and a need for attention and recognition. However, one thing is common; if these needs are not met the employee's motivation

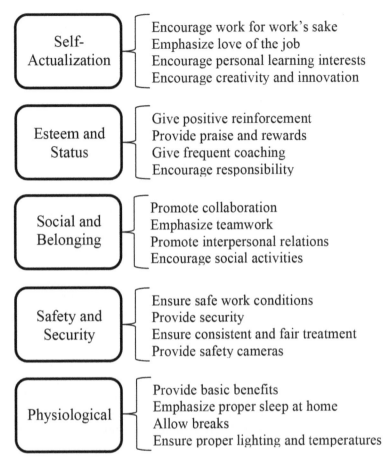

Figure 5.4. **Strategies for Motivating Employees Based on Human Needs**

will be affected. Understanding how to meet employees' human needs can help teacher leaders to be more effective.

The *two-factor motivation theory* proposed by Fredrick Herzberg (1966) is one of the more prominent theories of human motivation. Every teacher leader needs to understand this theory and how to apply it when motivating employees. While Herzberg primarily worked with industrial companies, his theories can also be applied to the education setting (see figure 5.5).

Herzberg's model is similar to Maslow's hierarchy and provides a basis for understanding human motivation. Herzberg concluded that people experience good or bad feelings based upon different types of conditions at work and their leadership. He theorized that different factors will influence motivation based upon workers' views toward these motivation factors.

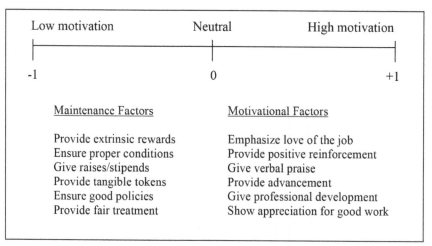

Figure 5.5.   Strategies Based on Herzberg's Two-Factor Motivation Theory

There were two predominant groups that Herzberg categorized his motivational factors—*maintenance* factors and *motivational* factors. *Maintenance* factors consisted of relationships with supervisors, peer relations, quality of supervision, administrative company policies, work conditions, and reward structures.

The maintenance factors were also called *extrinsic factors*. Extrinsic factors can be viewed as external types of rewards that can reinforce performance. For example, an employee may be motivated to accomplish a job task because of the desire for an extrinsic reward such as a bonus. This extrinsic factor, in essence, is the motivator that is stimulating the person to accomplish the task.

Motivational factors consist of work itself, the possibility of growth and advancement, responsibility, status within the organization, recognition, and achievement. Motivational factors are also called *intrinsic* factors. Intrinsic factors are significantly different in that the rewards are intangible.

Intrinsic factors are often obtained as a result of the work itself. For example, a teacher leader who has a love of education will be motivated in his or her job because of this *intrinsic* satisfaction. In the business world there are often people who are financially successful and could retire but they would rather continue working because they obtain fulfillment in life. Likewise, teachers who obtain satisfaction from work will be motivated to continue his or her growth and development and teaching career.

The *two-factor theory of motivation* can be applied to employees in a school. If an employee's maintenance factors such as school disciplines policies, the administration of the policies, safety and security, and school conditions are not met at a minimum level, employees can become dissatisfied and demotivated.

In other words, the lack of clear-cut school policies and inconsistent administration of the policies can result in people being dissatisfied and demotivated. Likewise, if an employee feels that the teacher leader is ineffective in providing basic work conditions and safety and security, the employee can also be demotivated.

Much like workers in a company, once *maintenance* factors have been met for employees within a school, in order to provide the opportunity for them to become more motivated, motivational factors must be provided. These intrinsic motivational factors might include potential for growth and learning, peer recognition, awards and work achievement, status within the school, and the rewards of future promotion opportunities. If motivational factors are not provided, employees may never become motivated to grow to higher performance levels.

The *expectancy motivational theory* is another landmark theory proposed by Victor Vroom (1964) that can be applied to the educational setting. Vroom theorized that human motivation is based upon the product of three factors: desire for reward (valence), belief that an effort will result in completion of a task (expectancy), and the knowledge that a reward will be obtained upon completion of the task (instrumentality).

When applied to the school setting, *valence*, the first factor, can be viewed as a person's preference for receiving a good performance rating (e.g., reward). The person may strongly desire a good rating and will be highly motivated to perform. However, if the person lacks this desire and is indifferent he or she will have a low valence and will not be motivated to achieve and will consequently lack the motivation.

The second level, *expectancy*, can refer to a persons' belief that his or her effort will result in the achievement of a desired task (e.g., successful completion of projects and work assignments). For example, if a person feels that higher quality work will result in a better performance rating, than the person will be motivated to work hard. However, if the person feels there is not a direct relationship between quality work and a positive rating, he or she will be less motivated.

The third level, *instrumentality*, relates to a person's belief that a reward can be realistically obtained. For example, the person might believe that the principal is prejudiced against him or her and no matter how well the person performs quality work, the person will never receive an excellent rating. In this case, the person's instrumentality will be low and the result will be a low motivation.

Highly motivated employees need to have high levels of all three factors: *valence, expectancy,* and *instrumentality.* Vroom theorized that the strength of a person's drive to reach a goal is based upon the combination of these three factors, and a leader should strive to provide incentives for people. Likewise, the experiences employees obtain in the organization can directly contribute to their drive for each of these factors. Teacher leaders can help provide these incentives by establishing work expectations and policies, fair and consistent evaluation, and proper reward structures (Webb, 2007).

The *equity motivation* model first proposed by Adams (1965) suggests that the motivation of people goes way beyond just satisfying their needs (see figure 5.6). This model suggests there is a direct relationship between how employees perform and how they value the rewards. Adams theorized that the issue of fairness applies to all types of rewards such as social, economic and psychological.

Outcomes (compared with others)	Inputs (compared with others)
▪ Pay/Benefits ▪ Special Rewards ▪ Psychological	▪ Work Effort ▪ Level of Work Difficulty ▪ Performance

Figure 5.6.   The Equity Motivation Model

The premise of this model is that people will bring input into their work (e.g., personal commitment, time, desire and energy) and expect to receive outcomes (e.g., money, praise, recognition and benefits). People will analyze the degree of fairness of receiving their own outcomes as compared to the outcomes being received by others. The fairness, or equality, of these factors will be subjectively judged by the person.

If the person believes that the *outcomes* (i.e., rewards) justify his or her degree of input and compared with others, than the person will be motivated. However, if the person feels that his or her outcomes are inadequate or unfair as compared to others, then the person will not be motivated. These feelings also can be reinforcing and become chronic.

For example, if an employee is contributing a high input but his or her performance rating is less than satisfactory as compared to his or her peers, an imbalance will result in the employee's mind. As a result, the employee may contribute less input to work and may openly complain and have a negative attitude.

Essentially the *equity motivational* theory explains that the motivation of a person is to avoid experiencing negative feelings that result from unjust treatment. These feelings result from the process of social comparison between people and coworkers. The work performance and rewards need to be in balance among workers.

It is important for teacher leaders to recognize that the reality of rewards may be different than the perception of the rewards. Employees often perceive rewards being higher to other people than themselves. The leader should recognize the equity motivation model in motivating people. In essence, the teacher leader needs to keep in touch with employees' feelings and help ensure rewards are given fairly and proportionately (Tomal, 2007).

BUILDING TEAMWORK AND ACCOUNTABILITY

Teamwork and accountability are synergistic characteristics of most organizations. Teacher leaders can serve an important role in helping an organization create a positive culture of working together and holding people accountable to achieve the vision of the school.

Tuckman (1965) identified several stages of team development. Teacher leaders can consider these stages of development in promoting positive teamwork within the organization. The four stages include *forming, storming, conforming,* and *performing.* During the *forming* stage this can be considered as the honeymoon stage.

In this first stage, employees are generally guarded, exchange pleasantries, and are somewhat respectful and cordial to each other. Employees assess their environment and the personalities and abilities of their coworkers. Employees also experience a degree of uncertainty regarding their relationships with their fellow coworkers and begin to formulate relationships.

In the second state, *storming,* conflicts emerge and coworkers may bid for power and rebel against their teacher leader as well as their fellow coworkers in an effort. The employees are attempting to find their place within the team and ranking within the unwritten social order. Employees who emerge as winners often develop informal power and leadership positions within the school.

The third stage is called *conforming,* and is sometimes referred to as the *norming* stage. This stage includes employees who establish standards of conduct and set norms for behavior. During this stage employees for the most part accept these rules and standards however may still lack open support of each other.

The last stage, called the *performing* stage, is when the group is a high functioning and proficient team. This stage allows group members to feel very supportive of each other, a sense of loyalty, and conflicts are managed constructively. This stage is the ideal one but often teams fail to reach this level and may function for years in a lower stage.

When the teacher leader is able to help a team achieve the highest level of performing, team members feel free to grow and learn new experiences. It is in this stage where the group functions most productively and efficiently.

The feelings of employees during this stage are positive toward each other. People generally have a sense of "we" and collaboration with each other. Much like a good sports team, the feelings toward each of the team members are cooperative and supportive as they all pursue a common goal.

The teacher leader can help the team members achieve the *performing* stage by establishing clear rules of conduct, a common purpose, trust and honesty, commitment, effective communications, appropriate conflict management, and recognition and reward systems. The leader is in essence the person who lays down the tracks and sets the example for the employees to follow.

The teacher leader cannot force the employees to become a high functioning team but can provide situations which allow the employees to achieve high performance, accountability, and teamwork. A teacher leader's ability to be proactive versus reactive is essential for building teamwork. *Proactive* leadership suggests the teacher leader's ability to anticipate the needs of employees, build trust, and take initiative in getting results (Mach, Dolan, and Tzafrir, 2010).

The *reactive* leader is one who is content with the status quo and does not have the foresight to anticipate employee needs and creates a working environment that is not vibrant and resourceful. A proactive leader is one who is also service-oriented. This leader recognizes his or her role as a leader in providing for the needs of others.

The notion of *servant leadership* is a moral value that entails a disposition of giving and altruism. The assumption that the leader is serving the needs of others is a key feature of moral and ethical leadership (Sergiovanni, 1990). The concept of moral leadership encourages learning that is based on moral and societal redeeming goals. For example, tennis players who serve for a game statistical have a better chance of winning the game. Like leadership, *those who serve often win.*

SUMMARY

The responsibility for leading and motivating employees is a responsibility of all teacher leaders. Teacher leaders need to be good role models and not only demonstrate effective values and leadership, but to also be able to employ leading and motivating strategies for building employee teamwork. Moreover, the ability to effectively coach and build a collaborative work environment is crucial for helping achieve the vision and goals of the school district.

The job of the teacher leader is one of effectively leading and motivating employees to achieve the school and departmental goals and is not to be taken lightly. Teacher leaders are in a position to make or break the morale and performance of new teachers and proper coaching can help to achieve success for all. Employing effective team building strategies can help motivate and develop a high-performing team.

CASE STUDY

DeKalb High Public School Staff Survey

You are a teacher leader at the DeKalb Public High School located in the northeastern United States. On the first day of the new school year your principal scheduled a meeting with you to present the results of a recent teacher and staff organizational survey. The results indicate that the areas of morale, communications, and teamwork are very low in your department.

In addition the principal thinks this might be affecting student morale and performance given that test scores have recently declined. Therefore, the principal has asked you to prepare a report regarding how you can address these issues. Prepare a two-to-three page report how you can address these issues including various strategies and techniques from this chapter.

EXERCISES AND DISCUSSION QUESTIONS

1. Explain the *teacher leadership capability model* that can be used for leading and motivated employees and how this model might be used to build teamwork and collaboration.
2. Incorporate Maslow's hierarchy or Herzberg's two-factor motivation theory in how you could motivate team members. Analyze your team members' performance and select specific strategies that might improve their performance and further motivate them.
3. Explain Tuckman's four stages for team development and list examples for building your own team at your school. Consider your own team and identify what stage your team is in, and what can be strategies you can do to help them perform at the highest level of teamwork.

REFERENCES

Adams, J. (1965). Inequity in social exchange. In L. Berkowitz (Ed.), *Advances in Experiential Social Psychology* (267–299). New York: Academic Press.

Hersey, P. (1994). *The situational leader*. New York: Warner Books.

Herzberg, F. (1966). *Work and the nature of man.* Cleveland, OH: World Publishing Company.

Mach, M., Dolan, S., and Tzafrir, S. (2010). The differential effect of team members' trust on team performance: The mediation role of team cohesion. *Journal of Occupational & Organizational Psychology, 83*(3), 771–794. doi:10.1348/096317909X473903

Maslow, A. (1943). A theory of motivation. *Psychological Review, 50,* 370–396.

McGregor, D. (1960). *The human side of enterprise.* New York: McGraw-Hill Company.

Nohia, N., Groysberg, B., and Lee, L. (2010). Employee motivation. *Harvard Business Review, 86* (7/8), 78–84.

Sergiovanni, T. (1990). *Value-added leadership.* San Diego, CA: Harcourt Brace Jovanovich.

Tomal, D. (2007). *Challenging students to learn: How to use effective leadership and motivation tactics.* Lanham, MD: The Scarecrow Press, Inc.

Tuckman, B. (1965). Developmental sequence in small groups. *Psychological Bulletin, 63,* 384–399.

Vroom, V. (1964). *Work & motivation.* New York: Wiley.

Webb, K. (2007). Motivating peak performance: Leadership behaviors that stimulate employee motivation and performance. *Christian Higher Education, 6*(1), 53–71. doi:10.1080/15363750600932890

Chapter 6

Communicating, Collaborating, and Evaluating

OBJECTIVES

At the conclusion of this chapter you will be able to:

1. Understand principles and techniques of communicating with employees (ELCC 1.2, 1.3, 3.2, ISLLC 1, 3, TLEC 1, 3, InTASC 2, 3, 7)
2. Understand strategies of listening and communicating with team members (ELCC 1.4, 1.5, 3.2, ISLLC 1, 3, TLEC 1, 3, InTASC 2, 7)
3. Develop skills in handling conflict and building collaboration with team members (ELCC 1.3, 1.4, 3.2, ISLLC 1, 3, TLEC 1, 3, InTASC 2, 3, 7)
4. Describe methods of conducting performance evaluations that are legally compliant (ELCC 1.4, 3.1, ISLLC 1, 3, TLEC 1, 3, InTASC 3, 7)

COMMUNICATING WITH TEAM MEMBERS

Motivating team members for high performance requires the use of effective interpersonal communication skills. The ability to talk with an employee and reach agreement so that both parties feel mutually satisfied is an ideal situation. For example, establishing quality interpersonal relationships between the teacher leader and team members is important for achieving academic success. Basic to establishing a good interpersonal relationship is the need to establish meaningful two-way communications.

Effective communication can be viewed as the process of encoding information, transmitting this information, and the receiving person decoding the information and responding. *Feedback* is important because it establishes and determines the quality of communication. This process can often occur almost instantaneously on a continuous basis between people.

Several *barriers* can impact the quality of communication among teachers and staff members. For example, the period of time when a teacher leader decides to talk to a staff member (i.e., timing of information), the environment in which the conversation takes place, the personal approach utilized, the method or medium used, and the actual selection of words and content all play an important part in the process.

For example, if a team member is emotionally upset and an issue arises in front of the team member's peers in a department meeting, the teacher leader should select another time in which to confront the situation rather than at that moment. Confronting the situation in this volatile situation may escalate the matter. The teacher leader may decide that the best time to address the problem might be after the meeting when they can be alone.

The *environment* plays an important part in the communication process. If a teacher leader is requested to discuss a motivational problem with a teacher in a formal office, a higher degree of stress and sense of importance will be established than selecting a more neutral location such as a hallway or cafeteria. If a teacher leader would like to address a motivation problem on a more informal basis, it may be more effective to select a more neutral location.

The *medium* that is used (i.e., method of communication), such as whether a teacher leader uses an email, one-on-one verbal discussion, telephone, or another person, affects the communication outcome. All these considerations should be taken into account by a teacher leader in deciding upon the best communication approach to use in communicating with team members about motivational matters.

Listening is another element of the communication process. Without *active listening* on the part of both the teacher leader and team member, the communication process will be hindered. The teacher leader must ensure that he or she is genuinely listening to an employee's position and must also ensure that the employee is listening as well.

Most people speak around 150 words per minute, although they are able to listen up to between 400 to 600 words per minute. With this mind, a listener's mind tends to wander, and he or she begins to think about other things while listening to a speaker. It is important that both parties pay close attention to each other. For example, the teacher leader may request an employee's full attention before initiating a discussion. Figure 6.1 illustrates typical irritating listening habits.

There are many barriers to effective listening such as interrupting the other speaker, never looking at the other person when listening or talking,

- ➤ Interrupting the person
- ➤ Never looking at the person
- ➤ Pacing back and forth
- ➤ Changing what the person says
- ➤ Fidgeting with a pencil or paper
- ➤ Finishing the person's statements
- ➤ Organizing papers

- ➤ Taking too many notes
- ➤ Answering a question with a question
- ➤ Showing a lack of interest
- ➤ Sitting too close to the person
- ➤ Postponing answering questions
- ➤ Intimidating the person
- ➤ Offending the person

Figure 6.1. Teacher Leader Irritating Listening Habits

not allowing the other person a chance to talk, continually fidgeting with a pencil or object, pacing back and forth impatiently, staring at the other person, continuing to wander off the subject, attempting to finish the other person's sentences, arguing with every point, or answering a question with a question. Poor listeners also may prejudge other individuals, daydream while listening, become bored, look uninterested, and forget the information in the discussion.

Good listeners look for areas of mutual agreement, keep an open mind, listen wholeheartedly, stay awake, and generally process the information that is being communicated.

For example, when a teacher leader is dealing with a team member, it might be easy for the teacher leader to make preconceived notions about the person, especially if he or she has had problems before. A teacher leader might prejudge the team member and develop a prejudice based upon these past experiences.

The teacher leader may not be open to genuinely listening to the staff member's point of view. The teacher leader may also have a tendency to abuse his/her authority. It is easier for a teacher leader to be directive when communicating with a staff member then to take the time to patiently engage in mutual, two-way discussion.

EFFECTIVE NONVERBAL COMMUNICATIONS

The use of *nonverbal communication* is also an important element when communicating with a team member. Many factors impact on nonverbal communication, such as proxemics, kinesics, and effective body language techniques. Nonverbal communications can sometimes be more powerful than verbal communications among faculty and staff.

Proxemics, which entails the principles and observations in the use of space as an extension of an individual's personality, can play a significant impact in resolving performance issues with team members. Some of the elements that affect proxemics might include the arrangement of furniture, physical distance between teacher and student, size and shape of a room, and physical appearance.

For example, the distance between the teacher leader and team member can impact on the interpersonal relations during the communication process. A distance of more than four feet between the team member and teacher leader indicates a more impersonal atmosphere. A more personal distance is generally about two to four feet between the two of them. A distance of less than two feet might create a very intimidating and hostile situation. While a teacher leader needs to consider these general proxemic parameters, cultural differences may change the distances.

The use of *kinesics* involves the study of body movements—postures, facial expressions, and gestures. Teacher leaders who exhibit power may use more stern gestures and direct eye contact. A more collaborative approach includes a relaxed posture, positive facial expressions, and open body gestures. While some teacher leaders may feel it is important to exhibit intimidating body language, this may have a negative impact on resolving a performance issue since team members may remain silent.

The teacher leader should also be aware of exhibiting defensive body language signals such as darting or glancing side to side, crossing one's arms in a rigid manner, or tensing body motions which can distract the team member from the discussion. See figure 6.2 for nonverbal strategies behavior to avoid when communicating with employees.

✓ Don't make defensive postures
✓ Don't look tense
✓ Don't evade the person's personal space
✓ Avoid bad eye contact
✓ Don't touch the person
✓ Avoid crossing your arms
✓ Avoid pointing your finger at the person
✓ Avoid steepling with your hands

Figure 6.2.   Nonverbal Behaviors to Avoid

EFFECTIVE VERBAL COMMUNICATIONS

There are several communication techniques that can be utilized when talking with a team member (see figure 6.3). For example, a teacher leader might utilize the technique of *paraphrasing*. Paraphrasing means to repeat back to the team member in the teacher leader's own words what the employee said. This helps to reinforce the point that the teacher leader is listening to the team member and ensure that the message was understood.

The use of *restatement* is a technique that can be used. Restatement means that the teacher leader repeats verbatim the team member's statement in an effort to encourage the person to continue talking. This can be viable technique to gain more information from team members, but it should not be overused since it can be viewed as prying and overly obtrusive.

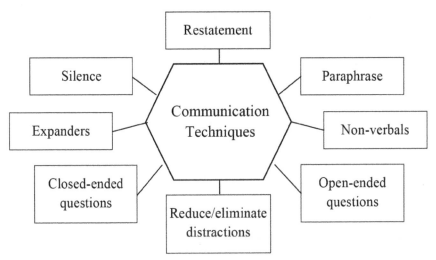

Figure 6.3. Communication Techniques

The teacher leader can use the techniques of open-ended and closed-ended questions. Open-ended questions cannot be answered by a simple yes or no and encourage the team member to continue talking. Open-ended questions usually involve words such as who, what, where, when, and how. The use of open-ended questions encourages the seeking of additional facts and information. Closed-ended questions can be effectively used when the teacher leader simply wants to obtain a yes or no answer. A simple phrase can yield a great bit of information and expedite the discussion.

The *silence technique* can be a very powerful technique when talking between two parties. Often when faced with silence, team members will talk. Using moments of silence in a skillful manner by the teacher can be a very valuable tool for opening up discussion and receiving more information from the team member. Silence can also demonstrate that teachers are generally willing to listen to the team member's concern and reduce or eliminate distractions during team conversations.

The use of *expanders* is a technique of stating simple comments such as "Go on," "I understand," "I see." Expanders encourage the team member to continue talking and have a reinforcing effect in establishing a mutual dialogue. A final technique includes the use of eliminating distractions within the room. A noisy environment hinders effective discussion. Finding a more suitable environment is critical to coaching a team member.

Communication Styles

An important factor that impacts upon the effectiveness of communication is the dominate communication style of people. Miscommunication often occurs when there is a difference in the communication styles between one person and another. The basis of communication styles was formulated by Carl Jung, a renowned psychoanalyst and student of Sigmund Freud. As an outgrowth of Jung's work on personality, four primary communication styles can be identified: the *intuitor, feeler, thinker, and doer*.

While each of us have and use all four styles, we tend to use one dominate style. The *intuitor* talks from a conceptual viewpoint and tends to communicate in the timeframe of the future. This person places an emphasis on creativity and originality. Intuitors often are wordy, ramble in their thoughts, and may be unrealistic and dogmatic. They look for unique and novel approaches to solve problems but tend to be unrealistic. When placed in stressful situations, they can be egocentric, condescending, and unorganized.

The *feeler* communication style is one who values feelings of other people. Feelers are good listeners and observers. To them, the feelings of people can often be more important than the results. They tend to be perceptive, patient, warm, and empathetic. Although they are people oriented, they can be impulsive, moody, overdramatic, and overly emotional. They also tend to operate out of the timeframe of the past.

While the communication style of a feeler has many positive attributes, feelers can be overemotional in a discipline situation. If a teacher leader has a predominant feeler style, he or she may overdramatize a team member's problem. Likewise, a team member who has a feeling style may more easily break down into tears.

The *thinker* communication style is objective, rational, and analytical. Thinkers can be effective in organizing thoughts and presenting them in a clear and logical manner. They can, however, be overcautious, rigid, and controlling. They tend to be indecisive in solving problems and would prefer to ponder rather than make a quick decision. Thinkers view things with respect to the past, present, and future timeframes.

Thinkers can come across as being too rigid given their desire to follow a structured, point-by-point format. They may be criticized as being overly detailed, long-winded, legalistic, and too business-like. Likewise, they can come across as being too methodical and micro-managing to team members.

The *doer* communication style is pragmatic and results-oriented. Doers act in the timeframe of the present. They are hard-driving and assertive. They can be, however, too short-term oriented in their thinking and may lack long-term considerations. They tend to be combative, act quickly, and sometimes impulsively.

The doer tends to be more concerned with the bottom line and communicates short and to the point. They are less likely to engage in personal and collaborative discussions with team members and are more concerned with railroading their opinions. As a consequence, they may come across to directive and bossy to team members.

The implications of communication styles are critical when dealing with motivational problems. People with similar styles tend to communicate more effectively with each other. They tend to *talk the language* of the other party. However, if both parties overuse their style, conflict can arise. For example, if two doers are talking, they may both become too forceful and insensitive to each other.

Problems in communication can arise when dealing with teachers who have a different style than the teacher. For example, if a teacher leader tends to be a doer and he or she is trying to motivate a team member who is predominantly a feeler, the teacher leader may appear to the team member as being overly assertive and lacking sensitivity. This situation can be annoying to the team member, and the team member may not listen. The person may view the teacher leader as intentionally belittling him or her and being disrespectful.

On the other hand, if the teacher leader has a thinker communication style, and the team member has a doer style, conflict may arise. The teacher leader may be viewed as too controlling, nitpicky, and impersonal. The team member may become frustrated and impatient and simply want to resolve the matter versus involving an in-depth and detailed discussion. The teacher leader may be viewed as one who is too structured and overly cautious and conservative.

The key to communicating effectively with a team member begins by identifying the teacher leader's own dominant style, then the style of the team member. This does not mean that the teacher leader must

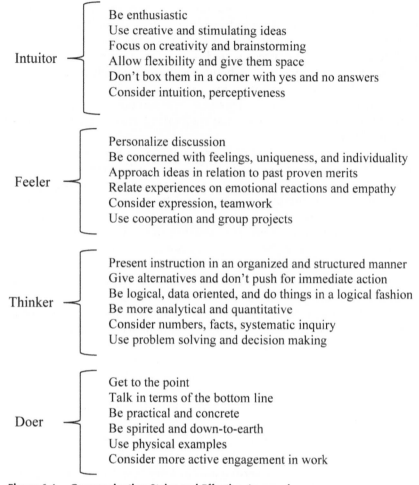

Intuitor
- Be enthusiastic
- Use creative and stimulating ideas
- Focus on creativity and brainstorming
- Allow flexibility and give them space
- Don't box them in a corner with yes and no answers
- Consider intuition, perceptiveness

Feeler
- Personalize discussion
- Be concerned with feelings, uniqueness, and individuality
- Approach ideas in relation to past proven merits
- Relate experiences on emotional reactions and empathy
- Consider expression, teamwork
- Use cooperation and group projects

Thinker
- Present instruction in an organized and structured manner
- Give alternatives and don't push for immediate action
- Be logical, data oriented, and do things in a logical fashion
- Be more analytical and quantitative
- Consider numbers, facts, systematic inquiry
- Use problem solving and decision making

Doer
- Get to the point
- Talk in terms of the bottom line
- Be practical and concrete
- Be spirited and down-to-earth
- Use physical examples
- Consider more active engagement in work

Figure 6.4.   Communication Styles and Effective Approach

permanently change but rather adapt his/her approach for the person. For example if the teacher leader is dealing with a team member who is a dominate feeler, the teacher leader should take extra time to personalize the discussion and be concerned with the person's feelings and emotions.

When approaching an intuitor, the teacher leader may be more dynamic and offer more creative and thought-provoking ideas. When dealing with a thinker, the teacher leader should structure the discussion in an organized and step-by-step approach. The thinker may also need more time to contemplate and process the discussion as compared to the doer who may be more inclined to quickly assess the bottom line.

Teacher leaders should get to the point with doers. However, it may be necessary to make sure the doer understands the details of the discussion when necessary. The teacher leader must balance the degree of accommodating the team member's style with his or her own style.

Communication styles, like learning styles, can have a dramatic impact on the teacher leader's ability to resolve conflict and foster collaboration and motivation. Recognizing and utilizing communication styles as a means to motivate team members for high performance (Tomal, 2013).

MANAGING CONFLICTS AND BUILDING COLLABORATION

One of the important aspects in motivating team members is the teacher leader's ability to manage conflict and building collaboration. Conflict is common among team members in schools. The teacher leader's ability to effectively manage conflict has a direct relationship with the motivation of team members and their performance.

Conflict can result from several sources: poor communications, roles, territorial issues, goal incongruence, stress, poor procedures and policies, and ineffective leadership. It is important for a teacher leader to identify the source of conflict before attempting to resolve it. Figure 6.5 lists some typical sources of conflict.

- Perceived favoritism to people
- Teacher demands upon employees
- Personality differences among staff
- Stress in person's life
- Outside home and social issues
- Politics and competition for power
- Change and new expectations
- School or work environment
- Miscommunication among people

Figure 6.5.   Examples of Sources of Conflict

The perception or actual favoritism given to team members by a teacher leader can be a demotivating factor for people. This perceived or real favoritism is a form of preferential treatment in the eyes of team members. Teacher leaders often are unaware of the perceived favoritism they may be giving to team members. The perception of favoritism can be as subtle as a mere lack of prolonged eye contact or the inflection of the teacher leader's voice to certain team members.

For example, a teacher leader may be more enthusiastic and positive to some team members, which can be perceived as favoritism in the eyes of others. Therefore, teacher leaders need to be aware of their communication and nonverbal behaviors toward all team members and ensure that they are done uniformly.

The personality differences among team members can also be a source of conflict. Team members' personality (e.g., intuitor, thinker, feeler, and doer) can be different and can lead to different preferences in approaching team exercises and also can lead to arguments. For example, if team members are working on a team project and one person who has a personality of a doer may be more aggressive in wanting to accomplish the project when working with a person with the thinker personality style. The thinker student may feel that the other student in being too pushy and short-minded concerning the project.

Likewise, the student's personality style of the feeler when working with the doer can cause conflict. The feeler may perceive the doer student personality as being insensitive toward him or her. Besides working in team projects, the normal interfacing among team members throughout the school day can also impact upon their motivation. Conflict can be the result of people with unlike styles.

Without a doubt, stress is common among team members in today's schools. There are high demands placed upon team members by parents, society, community, administrators, and peers, and so on. Also, team members' activities at home and in their social life can contribute a direct impact on conflict within the school. If a team member is experiencing difficulty at home, this can commonly be transferred to work.

The competition among team members for attention or power can contribute positively or negatively toward the team relationships. For example, if team members are competing among other people for a promotion, conflict may result. Likewise adapting to change can be another stressful event that can contribute to conflict among team members. Change is inevitable and those who fail to effectively manage change can have negative consequences upon their work relationships.

The school environment also contributes to a team member's motivation and attitude toward others. If the work environment has a great deal of noise and stimuli, the team member who does not adapt well to this environment may be more prone to conflict with other team members. The environment may be distracting to the person and his or her ability to focus on work can be hampered.

One of the contributors of conflict is that of miscommunication among team members. Human beings are social creatures and communicate on a daily basis. Each of their interactions often involves a negotiating element which leaves room for miscommunication to take place. For example, if a teacher leader makes a statement to a team member and it is misunderstood, the person may have ill feelings toward the teacher leader and become demotivated.

There are several different techniques for resolving conflict and building collaboration that can be utilized by the teacher leader. For example, figure 6.6 illustrates a *teacher leader–employee conflict needs model* that can be effective in understanding the underlying needs of conflict and coming to resolution. In the model, the degree of the teacher leader needs is illustrated on the vertical side of the model and the employee's level of needs is depicted on the horizontal side of the model.

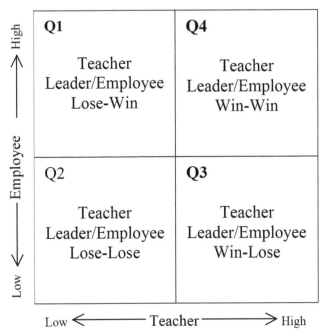

Figure 6.6. Teacher Leader-Employee Conflict Needs Model

Quadrant 1 is called the Teacher-Employee Lose-Win. This quadrant suggests that when the employee has a high degree of needs and the teacher leader has a low degree of needs a lose-win situation is created. In this case the employee may likely obtain needs at the expense of the teacher leader and resolution of the conflict is probably left unresolved.

Quadrant 2 is called the Teacher-Employee Lose-Lose. For example, if both the teacher leader and employee have low needs in resolving conflict, then the likely outcome may be a lose-lose situation (as illustrated in quadrant two of the model). This might be a situation where both the employee and teacher leader have disrespect toward each other and would rather avoid each other and resolving the conflict.

Quadrant 3 is called the Teacher Leader-Employee Win-Lose. For example if a teacher leader forces his or her needs to be met (e.g., high need level) at the expense of the employee's need (e.g. low) then a win-lose situation may arise. The conflict may go unresolved at the employee's expense. The teacher leader may be unaware that the conflict still exists unless the employee confronts the situation.

Quadrant 4 is called the Teacher Leader-Employee Win-Win. This is the ideal situation in resolving conflict. This quadrant suggests that both the teacher leader and employee have a high desire to accommodate their needs. In this situation a collaborative effort should occur with the employee and teacher leader having a desire to collaboratively resolve the conflict issue.

This situation often results in a win-win situation for both the teacher leader and employee and may be the best approach to use in attempting to resolve conflict. The essence of this situation is that through consensus the two parties can negotiate and come to a resolution that is the best for maintaining employee motivation and respect for the needs of the teacher leader and work environment.

There are several communication strategies a teacher leader can use to help resolve conflict and build collaboration. The use of the *anticipation* approach is especially good when dealing with one on one conflict. In this situation, if a teacher leader anticipates that a team member will have a negative response to a conflict issue, the teacher leader might begin by stating "I know we have had difficulty discussing this issue in the past, however you are very important and I did not mean any disrespect, so I was wondering if we could further discuss the situation."

By using the anticipation strategy the teacher leader, in essence, anticipates the team member's reaction in advance and tries to reduce the negative feelings the person might have. This can be effective technique in starting to build positive relationships. It can also serve to show that the person genuinely appreciates the other person.

The use of *paraphrasing* is a very common communication technique in which the teacher leader simply puts in his or her own words what the person is stating. For example, if an employee states that he or she is having difficulty with the content and feels uncomfortable in asking questions in department meetings, the teacher leader might state, "If you feel reluctant to talk in front of your peers because you may feel they will think poorly of you, I will be happy to work with you after the meeting."

In using this technique the teacher leader effectively paraphrases the employee's statements and reestablishes communication with the student.

Another technique, called *appeal to interests*, is a common one that can be used for one-on- one conflict resolution. A teacher leader might begin a conversation by identifying the team member's interest and using it to begin the conversation. This technique essentially personalized the conversation and sets the stage for discussing sensitive issues.

For example, if the teacher leader knows the team member enjoys sports, the teacher leader might start out by stating, "I know you enjoy sports, and I'm wondering how we can instill this same enthusiasm to our department." Introducing the student's interest in sports and hard work can help to bridge communication in resolving a motivational issue within the department.

An example of *limit setting parameters* is when a teacher leader states, "I can do this, but I can't do that." This allows the teacher leader to negotiate with the team members in resolving conflict but places a limit upon which resolution of agreement can occur. If the team member wants to achieve more time to complete a project, the teacher leader might say, "I can give you one more day, but I can't give you more than that." *Limit setting* is a good technique in introducing one's position and beginning the start of negotiations in resolving conflict.

In attempting to resolve conflict a teacher leader should always keep in mind the concept of the iceberg phenomena. Much like a real iceberg, where only the tip of the frozen material can be seen and a majority of the ice is underneath, so is it true for conflict between people. Often the presence of conflict is only indicative of underlying issues.

On the surface a team member may avoid a teacher leader; however, the real issues of conflict may be deep within. Therefore, a teacher leader should not just assume that the apparent issue is the only source of the conflict and should keep in mind to explore other issues that may be contributing to the conflict and building collaboration (Tomal, 2013).

CONDUCTING PERFORMANCE EVALUATIONS

In many school districts in the United States, performance evaluations are conducted by teacher leaders. These teacher leaders are often called teacher evaluators versus teacher coaches. For example, in the State of Illinois, all teacher evaluators must complete and pass the teacher evaluator training program, as provided by the *Performance Evaluation Reform Act* (PERA) of 2010 and Senate Bill 7 and articles 24A and 34 of the Illinois School Code.

Part of the evaluation must include an assessment of teacher performance and student growth. Key factors of this legislation include teacher evaluator proficiency, use of rubrics, performance standards, observation, collaboration, reflection, evaluation, and alignment of teacher performance to student growth.

In addition, performance evaluations have increased in use because of the emphasis on performance accountability and standards. Using the performance evaluation process can be an important tool in helping improve the performance of all teachers and staff within the school district.

There are many reasons for conducting performance evaluations (see figure 6.7). The performance evaluation should not be a single-purpose process whereby the teacher leader quickly completes a form, holds a brief appraisal session, files the form, and then goes back to business as usual. The teacher leader should not consider the performance evaluation as busy work or as a *compliance exercise* just to satisfy school district or legal requirements.

1. Provide performance feedback

2. Help motivate people

3. Promote communications

4. Use as a basis for staff development

5. Validate and document performance

6. Document performance problems

7. Comply with legal mandates

8. Provide rewards for people

9. Maintain fairness and accountability

Figure 6.7.   Reasons for Conducting Performance Evaluations

This feeling by teacher leaders may exist when evaluating tenured faculty. Some teacher leaders may feel handicapped in evaluating low-performing, tenured teachers when union contractual obstacles make it difficult to terminate a tenured teacher. Teacher leaders should not take the easy way out and complete a quick or shallow performance review.

Performance evaluations can be a mechanism for accomplishing many goals. One reason for the evaluation is to give genuine constructive performance feedback to the employee which can reinforce good performance and identify areas in need of improvement. The review session can also provide an opportunity to motivate employees through intrinsic verbal praise, and a basis for extrinsic rewards such as salary increases and bonuses.

The performance evaluation session can serve to help promote communications, review respective performance and develop continuous improvement plans for the future. This communication can serve as a basis for further developing people by establishing goals and gaining input that can help the entire organization (Prather-Jones, 2011).

Another reason for conducting the performance evaluation session is to validate and document performance of employees. This documentation serves as a record for employee performance which is needed when there is a need to terminate the employee in the future. Complying with legal and district policies is another reason to document performance problems. Lastly, the performance evaluation session can help to support personal accountability and provide a basis for financial rewarding employees.

While many people experience some anxiety during the performance review session, the benefits generally outweigh the time and effort. The performance evaluation session can provide an opportunity for documenting the employee's performance and serve as a system of fairness by informing employees how well they are performing in the organization.

There are many types of performance evaluation systems such as narrative appraisals, formative and summative assessments, 360 rating systems, and goal-based evaluations. Some organizations utilize an *open narrative evaluation*, especially for high-level administrators and managers. In this system the subordinate is asked to write a narrative regarding how well he or she performed during the year. This narrative is then used as a basis for performance review session. This type of system is a more informal approach and is infrequently used.

The *formative assessment* is often used to support the summative evaluation process. During the formative assessment informal feedback is given to the employee by the supervisor and this information is not used as part of the employee's permanent evaluation record. The whole idea of formative assessment is to give informal feedback without the fear of the information negatively impacting the employee's performance. However, it is sometimes difficult to entirely disregard the information when preparing a summative report.

The *summative evaluation* is the most popular approach and consists of a combination rating assessment and narrative section on the evaluation form. The evaluation forms can consist of a paper copy and filed in a cabinet or an electronic copy and stored in a computer. The *360 performance evaluation* is a system that uses a multirater feedback process to obtain an evaluation on an employee.

The 360 feedback is generally provided by multiple supervisors, peers, support staff, community members and possibly students. This system began during the 1950s in the corporate world and gradually gained popularity by human resources professionals. However, the system has been somewhat controversial in that it requires extensive time to collect the feedback and some people feel that the information is not always accurate or used exclusively for developmental purposes.

The traditional *combination rating* and *open-comment evaluation* is still probably the most popular rating form (Milanowski, 2011). The evaluation of an employee is generally conducted on a semi-annual or annual basis. Nontenured teachers are generally evaluated on a semi-annual basis and tenured teachers evaluated annually.

Conducting evaluations on a semi-annual basis provides a good opportunity to obtain regular feedback, although this can be time consuming for both the employee and teacher leader. Typically, the annual review is the requirement by school districts and state departments of education. Also the use of computer software has greatly increased the efficiency in completing and storing the evaluation forms into one database.

Regardless of the performance evaluation system used, there can be many problems associated with conducting the evaluation session (see figure 6.8). One problem is having sufficient time to prepare the form and

1. Poor preparation and hasty review

2. Leniency effect

3. Central tendency rating

4. Recency effect rating

5. Poor inter-rater reliability

6. Personal prejudice and bias

7. Game playing

8. Rater indecisiveness

9. Being overly judgmental or emotional

10. Being overly confrontational and directive

11. Conducting a shallow review

Figure 6.8. Problems Associated with Conducting the Evaluation Session

complete the review session. Conducting a shallow evaluation with an employee not only shows indifference, but may demotivate the employee.

The *leniency effect* occurs when a supervisor rates an employee too high in all the performance factors. This may happen when the supervisor desires to avoid dealing with potential employee dissatisfaction or resistance. The teacher leader may also overrate an employee to avoid creating conflict with the employee. *Central tendency* occurs when the supervisor rates all the performance factors in the middle of the scale.

One of the most difficult aspects in completing performance evaluation is to ensure that all teacher leaders strive to have a common understanding of what constitutes the performance standards of an employee, a term called *inter-rater reliability*. It is generally advisable that all teacher leaders participate in performance evaluation training to understand the criteria for rating employees and different levels of *standards of performance.*

Another problem with rating employees involves the human effect of harboring prejudice or bias toward an employee that may influence the rating. While the performance evaluation should be conducted objectively, it is nearly impossible exclude personal subjectivity. *Game playing* is another problem with performance evaluations which occurs when a teacher leader over or under rates an employee to support organizational politics.

For example, if a new teacher is being rated during the first six months the teacher leader may rate the new teacher lower to help protect himself or herself later should the teacher leader desire to terminate the new teacher for cause or deny the teacher tenure. The teacher leader may also rate an employee lower in order to allow the employee *room to grow*. All these examples are *game playing* and should be avoided.

The teacher leader should also avoid being too judgmental, emotional, directive, or controlling during the performance evaluation session. Other problems associated with conducting a performance evaluation include the following:

- Rating an employee based upon personal characteristics that violate discrimination laws
- Telling the employee about the rating or performance of other employees in the organization
- Changing a rating during the employee session because of undue pressure by the employee
- Conducting the session in a nonprivate location
- Focusing the appraisal review session on the supervisor's performance rather than largely on the employee
- Giving false promises to an employee to avoid conflict with the employee

- Rating the employee exceptionally high in an effort to gain the employee's favor and support
- Rating the employee low with the ulterior purpose of withholding a pay raise
- Overweighting of recent occurrences that are either favorable or unfavorable and omitting past performance

Most performance evaluation forms contain *performance rating levels* and *definitions*. For example, it is common to have *a five-level rating system* ranging from unacceptable to exceptional. Some forms have a three-rating level system consisting of not satisfactory, satisfactory and outstanding.

The Danielson Framework for Teaching model uses a rubric with four performance levels called unsatisfactory, needs improvement, meets performance and exceeds performance (Danielson, 2007). The Danielson model also outlines strategies on using the model for recruiting teachers, mentoring and induction, peer coaching, supervision, and evaluation. Use the performance evaluation form that has been approved by the district and state department of education.

Also several states of the United States have passed legislation outlining guidelines and requirements on teacher evaluation. For example, the State of Oregon passed legislation in 2012 that requires specific elements in evaluating teachers and administration. These elements consist of standards of professional practice, differentiated levels, multiple measures, evaluation and professional growth cycle, and alignment with professional learning (Oregon Department of Education, 2012).

Some evaluation forms may have a third section containing *performance goals*. The premise of including a *performance goals section* is to support the achievement of the school improvement plan initiatives and goals of the school district. In this case, teacher leaders would write performance goals for the ensuing year. The idea of writing goals helps to document performance expectations, promote communications, and contribute to the overall employee's development.

Many school districts connect the performance goals to the district teaching framework. For example, the goals could be written to support the domains of the teaching framework: Planning and preparation, classroom environment, instruction, and professional responsibilities (Danielson, 2007). The State of Ohio has adopted a goal-setting process that incorporates a self-assessment and analysis of student data (Ohio Teacher Evaluation System, 2011).

The format for writing goals, regardless of the type of teaching framework, are often based on SMART criteria, which are *specific* (describe results to achieve), *measurable* (clearly written and state a level of achievement expected), *agreed upon* (are agreed upon by the teacher leader and employee), *realistic* and *relevant* (are challenging, flexible and achievable and provide stretch for the employee), and *timely* (are attainable within specified period of time).

An example of a SMART goal might be "to increase the student achievement performance in the school by 10% as measured by the state standards-based achievement test by end of the school year." In addition to having professional SMART goals that are based on the operation of the school, it is common to have *personal development goals*, which are goals that help support the development of the employee.

In essence there are two types of goals, *professional development* that related specifically to achieving the initiatives of the organization, and personal development goals that help the employee growth. Examples of these goals for an administrative position include the following.

Professional Development Goals

1. Reduce student absenteeism by 10 percent by year-end.
2. Improve test scores by 5 percent.
3. Develop a strategic community business program.
4. Develop a school crisis management program.
5. Purchase, install and provide training for using SMART boards in technology classrooms.

Personal Development Goals

1. Improve writing skills.
2. Learn a new software program.
3. Improve time management skills.
4. Improve leadership skills.
5. Improve stress management.

Figure 6.9 lists the typical steps for conducting the session. Every school district should provide sufficient training and guidelines in conducting the performance evaluation for all teacher leaders. The *preparation for the performance evaluation session* should be thorough, step 1. It is important to schedule sufficient time and a location that is private and without distractions.

Generally it is advisable for the employee to complete a self-assessment prior to the session. The employee can either send this self-assessment in advance to the supervisor or bring it to the evaluation session. The advantage of sending the self-assessment in advance allows the teacher leader to anticipate the employee's evaluation although it might bias the teacher leader's own rating of the team member.

---

1. Prepare appraisal form (and schedule logistics for session)

2. Introduce session (set stage, rating criteria, and overview)

3. Review performance evaluation ratings (for each section)

4. State the overall rating

5. Obtain employee's reaction and discuss development areas

6. Obtain employee's signature on form

7. Discuss and agree on next year's goals (optional)

8. Document and file performance evaluation form

Figure 6.9.   Steps in Conducting the Performance Evaluation

In step 2 the teacher leader *introduces the session* by providing an overview for the process, establishing expectations, criteria for ratings and essentially sets the stage for the performance appraisal session. Step 3 involves the supervisor *reviewing all the performance ratings* for all the sections on the form. Generally, a teacher leader reviews each of the ratings and then gives and *overall rating* at the end, step 4.

However, it is possible that the teacher leader may want to give the overall rating prior to reviewing each of the rating sections. This might be the case when there is an outstanding employee and by giving the overall rating in advance may help to reduce anxiety and allow for a more constructive discussion. When evaluating a poor performer it is advisable to give the overall rating at the end so the teacher leader can build justification for the rating, especially if the employee needs to be placed on probation.

After the rating has been given it is often good to obtain the *employee's overall reaction* and then discuss general *development areas*, step 5. It is critical to *obtain the signature* of the employee on the performance appraisal form, step 6. The signature does not indicate that the employee agrees to the form but acknowledges that the form has been reviewed with the employee.

Also an optional step in the session might be for the teacher leader to *discuss next year's goals* and agree upon the goals with the employee, step 7. In this case the teacher leader may request that the employee prepare in advance and bring these goals to the session. This approach can help expedite the process and avoid the need for another meeting.

The performance evaluation session concludes by *documenting and filing all forms* in accordance with district policy, step 8. In the event that follow up is needed for employees who may be placed on probation, then a schedule would be developed. Also, it is important that the forms be sealed and held confidential to protect the employee and institution.

Critical to the performance evaluation session is adhering to federal, state, and school district laws and policies. There are several laws and potential union contract agreements that need to be understood by teacher leaders before administering the performance appraisal session. All employees need to understand these laws and a copy of them should be displayed on the institution's bulletin board and website.

Most federal laws include additions to the *Civil Rights Act of 1964*, which prohibits against discrimination on the basis of race, sex, religion, national origin, color, and certain medical conditions. The teacher leader should make sure to restrain from noting any performance that reference any of these factors that could be construed as discriminatory.

For example, a teacher leader should not rate a female employee lower just because she is pregnant. Another law that may impact the appraisal is the *Age Discrimination Act of 1967*, which prohibits age discrimination beginning at 40. A teacher leader should avoid comments such as "Nice job for an old man," or "You need to get with it and get out of the dark ages and learn technology like the young teachers."

Also, negative comments based on age can not only be hurtful to an employee, potentially illegal, and a violation of the institution's values and code of conduct. Also, statements regarding people's lifestyle, if irrelevant to the employee's performance or institution's codes of conduct, should be avoided. There is difficulty in discerning actual age discrimination and local school counsel should always be consulted.

Another law that may impact a performance evaluation session is the *Americans with Disabilities Act of 1990*, which prohibits discrimination on the basis of actual, previous or perceived mental or physical disability. A teacher leader should demonstrate caution in rating a disabled employee if reasonable accommodations have not been provided which could have improved his or her performance.

The *Title VII, Section 1604, Sexual Harassment Law* may also apply during the performance appraisal session. A teacher leader may genuinely express concern for an employee and may want to show support by giving the employee a hug or by embracing the employee. The teacher leader should restrain from touching the employee in any manner other than perhaps a handshake.

While the teacher leader may have good intentions, these types of actions may be construed to be sexual harassment behaviors and should be avoided. The teacher leader should be careful in the choice of works and avoid terms such as "honey," "cutie," "good girl," "you're a good boy," or other gender based statements that could be somewhat belittling and disrespectful and potentially violate sexual harassment laws.

Another federal law that may impact the evaluation session is the *Family Medical Leave Act of 1993*. This law prohibits discrimination against employees who request time off for their own serious illness or a family member. This law may have implications in giving a performance rating to an employee, especially if the rating is less than satisfactory when the performance might have been an approved leave of absence by the employee. These types of performance issues are not always clear-cut and demand careful thought by the teacher leader.

Other potential problems may be impacted by union agreement. For example, a contractual agreement may allow an employee to request a third party to be present during an evaluation session, especially when the evaluation is anticipated to be unfavorable to the employee.

SUMMARY

The proper supervision and communications with team members requires a systematic and comprehensive knowledge human resource management. Understanding the myriad of state and federal laws and local school policies is critical in leading and coaching employees. The proper mentoring and coaching of employees can help improve student achievement and contribute to high morale in the organization.

Moreover, conducting effective performance evaluations can help ensure that team members perform to the standards required by the organization and allow the school district to remain legally compliant. The legal considerations must always be a top priority for teacher leaders.

There are numerous resources available to assist teacher leaders in this entire process and should be utilized to develop the best systems and processes that are relevant for an organization. Moreover, developing a collaborative approach with involvement by team members can help to ensure agreement and success in producing high-performing team members.

CASE STUDY

Madison High School Science Department Strategic Goals

You have been recently been promoted as a teacher leader for the Science Department at Madison High School in northwestern United States. The school principal has asked you to submit department strategic goals that can improve communications, reduce conflict among department teachers, and improve morale and collaboration in the department. Prepare a two- to three-page strategic action plan for achieving this request.

EXERCISES AND DISCUSSION QUESTIONS

1. List and describe some of the relevant federal, state, and school laws and policies impacting the evaluation of teachers.
2. List the characteristics of an effective teacher leader when communicating with department employees.
3. Describe some major methods to reduce conflict and build morale and motivation of department members.

REFERENCES

Danielson, C. (2007). *Enhancing professional practice: A framework for teaching*. Alexandria, VA: Association for Supervision and Curriculum Development.

Hanson, S. (2010). What mentors learn about teaching. *Educational Leadership, 6*(8), 76–80.

Milanowski, A. (2011). Strategic measures of teacher performance. *Phi Delta Kappan, 92*(7), 19–25.

Ohio Teacher Evaluation System. (2011). http://www.education.ohio.gov

Oregon Department of Education. (2012). http://www.ode.state.or.us

Prather-Jones, B. (2011). Some people aren't cut out for it: The role of personality factors in the careers of teachers of students with EBD. *Remedial & Special Education, 32*(3), 179–191.

Tomal, D. (2013). *Managing human resources and collective bargaining*. Lanham, MD: Rowman & Littlefield Education, Inc.

Chapter 7

Managing Change

OBJECTIVES

At the conclusion of this chapter you will be able to:

1. Understand the role of the teacher leader as a change agent (ELCC 3.3, ISLLC 3, TLEC 1, 3, InTASC 2, 3, 7)
2. Articulate the obstacles to implementing change (ELCC 3.3, ISLLC 3, TLEC 1, 3, InTASC 2, 3, 7)
3. Understand organizational structures, the various roles and purposes of leadership, and ways to promote the success of students by leading all stakeholders in the change process (ELCC 1.4, 1.5, 2.1, 2.4, 3.1, 4.1, 4.2, 4.3, ISLLC 1, 2, 3, 4, TLEC 1, 3, InTASC 2, 3, 7)
4. Understand processes to engage and motivate faculty, staff, and community members to establish collaboration, communication, and organizational capacity to implement and sustain change for school improvement (ELCC 2.1, 2.2, 2.3, 2.4, 3.1, 3.2, 4.2, 6.1, 6.2, 6.3, ISLLC 1, 2, 4, 6, TLEC 1, 3, InTASC 2, 3, 7)
5. Describe ways to build and sustain positive relationships with all stakeholders involved in the change process to promote shared leadership. (ELCC 1.1, 1.2, 1.4, 1.5, 2.1, 2,4, 3.1, 4.1, 4.2, 4.3, ISLLC 1, 3, 4, 5, TLEC 1, 3, InTASC 2, 3, 7)

THE NEED FOR CHANGE

Schools are routinely challenged to establish goals and objectives, operate efficiently, increase student performance, and create reward systems for employees. All of these challenges require change. For more than a decade we have been deluged with negative reports on our schools. In part, this is due to the over reliance on standardized performance measures required under No Child Left Behind (NCLB).

NCLB focused on the importance of teachers being well educated and knowing their subject, resulting in the current focus on highly qualified teachers, National Board Certification, evaluation, performance, and teacher preparation programs. It was an attempt at change schools through legislation. Whether it has worked has been both a function of the willingness and ability of teachers and schools to change.

Under NCLB almost no school district is immune from failure. The fact is that there are signs of both excellence and mediocrity. Contrary to popular belief, U.S. students generally outperform students from other large countries on international assessments of basic literacy. At the same time, however, millions of students attend school each day in crumbling facilities and many of the country's poorest urban and rural areas attend schools that lack even the barest necessities.

With respect to change, the question is not how the nation's public schools are performing in relationship to the past but what will be our path in the future. Will it be one of excellence or one of mediocrity? And, if the country chooses excellence, what is it that we value as excellent and how do we change our schools and school systems to get there?

How does the educational system develop change leaders and how do we actually implement and execute change in our schools in the future? Will the political bureaucracy that created NCLB lead educational change, or will innovation and change come internally from educational stakeholders such as teachers and teacher leaders?

More than 14,000 school systems in the United States serve 80,000 public schools, employ 2.5 million teachers, and serve 44 million public school students. Within this universe, there are incredible extremes. New York City, with more than one million schoolchildren, is so populated that it would rank thirteenth nationally in student enrollment if it were a state. In contrast, the entire state of Nebraska has about 1.6 million residents but 662 school districts. More than half of these districts consist of a single elementary school. With all this diversity, are teacher leaders an important resource for driving and executing change?

Any discussion of change in schools must include a debate over the future direction of leadership. More and more schools are utilizing teachers to promote collaboration, teamwork, and decision making from the bottom up (Wynne, 2001). Effective teacher leaders identify areas for classroom improvement. They initiate, implement, and sustain change in the classroom. They promote change as a means for continuous instructional improvement.

There are many existing models for school change. Most of these focus on systemic changes in organizations. They do not, however, usually emphasize the most important change agents in schools—teachers. These models often talk about change from the "top down" not from the "bottom up." They do not generally address the role of teacher leaders. Teacher leaders can cultivate grass roots changes in the learning systems of schools.

Change can be driven by many sources. These would include changes in legal requirements such as state or federal laws, goals, strategic plans, staff initiatives, parental concerns, demographics, and availability of financial resources. Figure 7.1 shows the change drivers for schools.

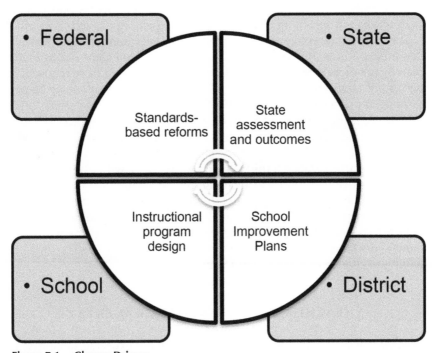

Figure 7.1. Change Drivers

One of the common elements of change in school systems is that it is often brokered. School districts are subject to a myriad of rules and regulations. Collective bargaining agreements often dictate that change must be negotiated. When the participants cannot agree on the type and rate of change there can be dire consequences. A recent example of brokered change through negotiation is the 2012 Chicago Teachers Union strike. The strike was the first one in twenty-five years, and other than compensation, the key issues were changing the method of teacher evaluation, which ties teachers' ratings to the growth and achievement of their students, and a longer school day. Mayor Rahm Emanuel noted that "the settlement was an honest compromise" and "a new day and new direction for the Chicago Public Schools" (Rossi et al., 2012, p. 1).

Likewise, state and federal regulations often dictate change at the local level. NCLB and Race to the Top (RTTT) are both examples of the federal government's attempts to change the educational system from the top down. Have they been successful? At this juncture, the jury is still out. While almost everyone would agree that the goals of NCLB were noble, almost all educators believe that the goals and/or timelines producing measurable outcomes were unrealistic.

On a state-by-state basis the criteria for student success and teacher performance differ. Some thirty-three states have approved waivers of NCLB. Some states have set performance goals at different levels for various subgroups of students. In Florida, Governor Scott came out against a plan by the Florida State Board of Education that would have required 86 percent of white students but only 74 percent of black students to be performing at proficient levels by 2017–18 (*Daytona Beach News Journal*, 2012).

What does the future hold for educational change in America's schools? Arnie Duncan, speaking about his second term as the U.S. secretary of education said that he "will use his second term to continue to leverage education improvement at the state and local levels, with a new emphasis on principal preparation and evaluation" (McNeil, 2012, p. 1). Duncan went on to say that he thought that district level innovation is important. So with the pressure on local school systems, all stakeholders must be willing to reevaluate and reallocate resources to improve student achievement and graduation rates. In other words, local school systems must be willing to change in a meaningful way.

TEACHER LEADERS AS CHANGE AGENTS

Teacher leaders are in a unique position. They are expected to be change agents for instructional improvement as well as coaches and mentors for teachers. As resources have become scarcer, schools have come to depend on teacher leaders as a means of implementing change through pedagogy as opposed to a commitment to provide more resources.

To be effective, teacher leaders need the staffs that they supervise or coach to invest in the changes they are advocating. In other words, there has to be some intrinsic or extrinsic reason for them to make that investment. Intrinsic reasons would include student motivation and achievement, citizenship, compassion, ethics, and so on. Extrinsic reasons would include items such as competitiveness, standardized tests, class rank. Unfortunately, with so many states tying teacher evaluation to student performance, it is hard not to focus on student testing.

Teacher leaders must recognize that "ownership" is both a blessing and curse. The same reason that change agents want the teachers they coach to buy in to a process can prevent them from seeing failure. For example, take the case of class size. For whatever reason, most teachers believe that lower class size equates to student achievement. Unfortunately, the body of research on class size neither supports nor refutes that assumption. If teachers recognized this, they might be more open to trading class size for coaching, mentoring, and professional development

Types of Change

There are two types of change: first-order or surface change that impacts components of an organization and second-order or systemic change that impacts the entire organization. The role of the teacher leader as a change agent is different depending on which type of change is being implemented.

First-order change may lead to more systemic change but it is incremental in nature (Stivers and Cramer, 2009). An initiative to improve student self-esteem in a classroom, a pilot program to test a new math strategy, or a new course in the curriculum are all examples of first-order change. All these examples are areas in which teacher leaders provide direction.

Second-order change is, by its very nature, systemic change. Implementing Common Core initiatives across a school district would be an example of a second-order change. Moving a high school to a small learning community (SLC) model would be another. These types of changes require a change in beliefs and culture. These are large-scale changes for the organization.

Waters, Marzano, and McNulty (2003) aligned twenty-one leadership practices that were required for first- or second-order change to take place. What they found is that for first-order change to take place there had to be a sense of collaboration, well-being, and solidarity among staff. Second-order change, however, required that staff develop a shared vision.

Teacher leaders can be proponents for either first- or second-order change. Their roles, however, are quite different. They would tend to be more experimenters when it comes to first-order change. They would look for ways to help teachers address the specific needs of their students. These might include looking for materials, resources, professional development, and/or small-scale grants.

For large-scale changes to the organization, teacher leaders would most likely take on more of a cheerleader approach. The focus would tend to be on groups of teachers as opposed to working with teachers individually. In implementing second-order change, teacher leaders are often implementing change where outcomes have already been prescribed.

Estimating the degree of change is sometimes difficult. One needs to take into account whether the change will be perceived as first- or second-order change, what stakeholders will be affected, and how divergent the change is from their current beliefs. Stakeholders could include teachers, parents, and/or students.

The Teacher Leader Role in Change

Teacher leaders are not always in a management position where they have the authority to dictate curricular, instructional, or assessment system changes. There is a fine line that teachers must walk between being a coach and a manager. Teacher leaders must create a culture where leadership is distributed. The role is not so much that of a traditional "leader" but someone who models good practices and works collegially to implement them.

For teacher leaders the goal is to increase effectiveness and capacity though enhanced classroom practices. To do this teacher leaders must be committed to a learning organization. Trust, collaboration, teamwork, risk taking, continued improvement, and professional development are all indicators of a learning organization.

Fink and Resnick (2001) note that school improvement depends on principals who can operate in a complex, changing society. Never has the time been riper for change leaders than right now. If operating in a culture of change is important to principals, it is equally important to teacher leaders (see figure 7.2).

Teacher leaders need to focus on student learning as their central change focus. Schools are complex organizations. Attempting to promote too many changes at one time may lead to overload and fragmentation. That is not to say that there can't be change within the change. Teacher leaders should always be looking to achieve greater alignment. It is their job to address the hard-to-solve problems.

Content coaches offer teachers the kind of professional development that research says is most effective: ongoing, high quality, and focused on instruction. This type of professional development gives teachers ongoing feedback and supports collaboration. The key is for teacher leaders to encourage teachers to explore other ways of doing things. This requires that teachers have time reflect on how they teach.

Change coaches focus on first- and/or second-order change implementation. As schools experience challenges from Common Core, leading them toward meaningful improvement has never been more critical. Once upon

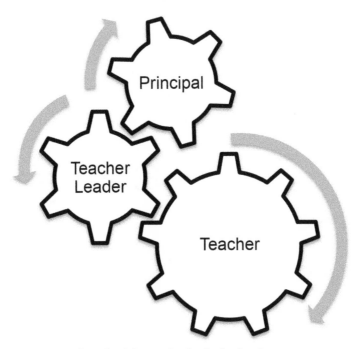

Figure 7.2. The role of the teacher leader in the change process

a time, a school leader was usually the principal who tried to maintain the status quo. Now, entire leadership teams, including teacher leaders, are expected to react to local, state, and federal legislative expectations.

In order to be effective change coaches, teacher leaders need to broaden what counts for effective learning beyond academic achievement. This would include areas such as student engagement, participation, and self-concept and human capital. The Japanese, for example, have very different goals from those most talked about in the American educational arena.

First, human relations skills are considered essential for the educated person. Second, the Japanese view academic knowledge as just one part of the more comprehensive goal of developing *ningen* (human beings). This idea of ningen assumes a holistic approach to growth and learning. Can these same goals be applied to American schools to drive change and excellence?

Change Skills for Teacher Leaders

There are a number of skills needed by teacher leaders to effect change. They fall into two basic categories: *leadership* and *pedagogical* (see figure

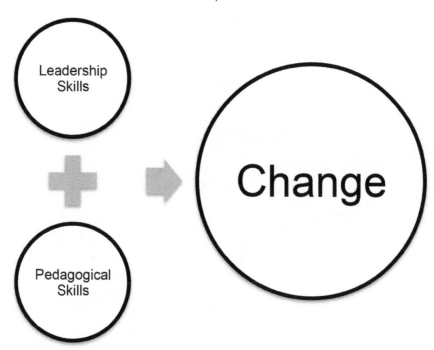

Figure 7.3.   Skills for Promoting Change

7.3). The leadership model that seems to embody all of the roles of the teacher leader is the *shared leadership model.* Shared leadership requires leaders to be collaborators, facilitators, and decision makers. Unless teacher leaders have formal power to evaluate and recommend retention, their ability to lead will be dependent on their likeability and expertise.

One form of shared leadership is *distributed leadership.* It not only creates opportunities for teamwork but expanded participation by all teachers. Teacher leaders who invoke distributed leadership do so by assigning tasks to many individuals in a meaningful way. This is a vastly different approach from the traditional "volunteer" approach where often only a few strong teachers exercise their leadership skills.

Obviously, not all individuals are going to be receptive to change. Evans (1996) and Senge (1999) both observed that an individual's predisposition to change will depend on how they see the change—will it result in growth or loss. For teachers who are struggling and recognize it, a change may be seen as an opportunity. For teachers who are currently successful and their students are achieving, this may be seen as in intrusion into their domain.

Teacher leaders must develop skills that address and support individual needs during change. The leader needs to be empathetic to the fact that change can be painful. It is loss, growth, and trust building all rolled into one process. Teacher leaders who successfully navigate teachers' human needs during change will increase the organizations ability to tolerate change.

Pedagogical skills include the concepts of collaboration, demonstration, coaching, and mentoring. These are skills that relate to the implementation of change and are equally effective with individuals or groups. The purpose of *collaboration* is not only to build teamwork but also to explore new ways of improving how things are done. Collaboration is a powerful skill. When it works, change will take place on its own without coercion or prompting.

Another skill is *demonstration.* Teachers need to be able to compare what they are doing with best practices on a regular basis. Of course, this means that teacher leaders have to be ahead of the curve with respect to best practices or be willing to utilize members of their team to demonstrate key concepts. Showing teachers how to engage in a Socratic dialogue would be an example of demonstration.

Monitoring processes, measuring progress and emphasizing positive outcomes are all traits of a good coach. Coaching for change requires that teacher leaders have the ability to identify gaps in performance. Coaching involves using the right "players" in the right positions as well as coaching the right skill sets for that position.

Mentoring is a skill set that many believe simply comes with longevity and expertise. But just because someone is a brilliant teacher in the classroom doesn't make him or her successful with adult learners. Mentoring requires a certain nonjudgmental attitude. It requires an individual who can differentiate between failure and success and the impact of both.

EXECUTING CHANGE—TRENDS AND CHALLENGES

Tomal, Schilling, and Trybus (2013) identified eight *commonalities for change.* They are universal challenges that all educators, including teacher leaders, will face in the future. Teacher leaders will play an integral part in addressing these challenges. The commonalities include both first- and second-order change. They also have implications for implementing change within the organization. It is important that teacher leaders understand these concepts and the challenges they present. It is also imperative that teacher leaders understand the impact of the commonalities on their role (see table 7.1).

The first commonality is the creation of a *human-centered school environment.* School environment reflects the culture, climate, and leadership of the school. Human relation skills and teamwork are essential if schools

Table 7.1.   The Commonalities for Change and Impact on the Roles of Teacher Leaders

Commonality for Change	Impact on Role of Teacher Leaders
Human-centered school environment	Distributed leadership
Desire to excel	"Stretching the mindset"
Business intelligence	Data coach
Sense of urgency	Prioritize
Edu-entrepreneurship	Teacherpreneur
The impact of technology	Productivity
Incentivizing innovation	Risk taker
Planning for a global future	Visionary

are to seek excellence. The key to executing change is creating a climate in which the staff believes, "They did it themselves." To do this, there needs to be a human-centered school climate. Simply using task forces, committees, teams of professionals, and professional learning communities is not enough.

Good change leadership promotes order as opposed to control. In other words, change leadership is about leading, not managing. It liberates staff to implement change. Creating a climate that builds human networks and motivates staff is a key to excelling.

The second commonality is the *desire to excel*. Staff is not going to strive for something they can't appreciate, don't think is possible, or don't care about. Since excellence can be a moving target, teacher leaders must establish both short- and long-term benchmarks. These benchmarks need to be measurable in terms of effectiveness and efficiency. For educators one of the biggest challenges in defining excellence is what can be referred to as "stretching the mindset."

As a teacher leader, it is important to stretch the mindset of staff from focusing on the status quo to the future. One way to do this is to have challenging definitions of excellence. Challenge staff to excel. Whether educators like it or not, one result of NCLB was a set of challenging definitions of excellence. No group or subgroup was left out when pursuing excellence.

The third commonality is the use of *business intelligence*, which consists of metrics and dashboards to improve student performance and resource allocation. Data-driven decision making in schools is a relatively new occurrence in education compared to the private sector. Data processing software is now just catching up to the demand for information in schools. Unfortunately, most of the software that is currently available still doesn't meet most districts' needs.

In the not too distant future, it will be possible to correlate an individual student's achievement with human resource and financial data. How would the role of a teacher leader change if they could prescribe a teacher for a student—in other words, match a teacher's instructional style with a student's learning style?

For teacher leaders, real-time metrics and benchmarks that measure the direct impact of strategies and provide performance monitoring are essential. They enhance the ability of teacher leaders to make data-driven change and decisions. For example, they assist in identifying at-risk students, making evaluations, communicating results to parents, identifying real-time where interventions can take place and assist in the allocation of human and financial resources.

The fourth commonality is the development of a sense of urgency. A sense of urgency is, at times, very clear. For example, let's say that the state passes legislation requiring that Common Core curriculum be used in every school by June 30. In this example, the state has defined both the urgency and the parameters. In other instances, however, teacher leaders will not have a clear vision of what needs to be done or when it needs to be done. In those instances, the teacher leader needs to identify a process for determining not only what needs to be changed, but also the urgency of the change (see figure 7.4).

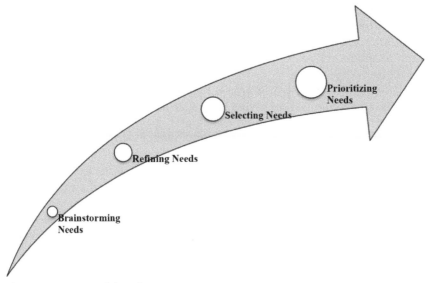

Figure 7.4. Determining Change Urgency

In most organizations there are more needs than the available resources can support. Too often, schools and school districts try to tackle too many changes at the same time. This action results in capital—both human and financial—being spread too thin. The result is unfulfilled needs, failure, and unrealized change. Furthermore, if repeated year after year, it leads to staff complacency. For this reason, it is essential that organizations focus on just a few significant changes that become the focus of the organization and align with the mission and vision of the school district.

The fifth commonality is the development of edu-entrepreneurs. Edu-entrepreneurs are both change agents and change leaders. Edu-entrepreneurs are individuals who are idea generators. They look for new links, have investors willing to buy into change, and most importantly, take risks. They look to exploit change.

Every business, including education, gets a makeover sooner or later. There are many reasons why this may occur. Berry and the Teacher Solutions 2030 Team (2011) found that there are *teacherpreneurs* operating throughout the education system. These entrepreneurial roles for teachers have big implications for teacher leaders. They are teacher leaders, but without the labels described earlier—such as coach, mentor, department chair. *Teacherpreneurs* are teachers who teach who also happen to be leaders.

The sixth commonality is the *impact of technology*. Technology can play a significant role in not only increasing productivity at every level of the education system, but also in driving change. Technology can also be used to monitor and implement change. There are a number of open-source project management programs that school personnel can use to track complex plans. These open-source programs include Gantt, Program Evaluation Review Technique (PERT) charts, and Work Breakdown Structure (WBS) charts.

There are also free open source survey tools to collect data from staff, parents, and students. Free online tools such as *Cacoo* (2012) that allow the creation of block diagrams, flow charts, and mind maps. With this tool a group of employees can be online simultaneously so that the process of ideation, brainstorming, and discussion is encouraged.

The seventh commonality is *incentivizing innovation*. To be effective, teacher leaders must examine a multitude of models and strategies that create incentives to implement change in their schools. They must commit to providing the resources for faculty to acquire new skills. The status quo is changing rapidly. In fact, one thing is very clear. Change is occurring as rapidly in schools as technology is changing daily life. Moreover, depending on the viewpoint, school achievement data are becoming so transparent that every initiative, every teacher's performance, and every student's success or failure is under public scrutiny. If meaningful change is to be achieved, all stakeholders must be involved in the evolution of the organization in an active way.

Future successes may lie in a mindset that rewards successes and innovation but does not penalize staff for risk taking and failure. Teacher leaders must provide teachers with better information so they can act now regarding decisions that will affect students in the future. How can teacher leaders encourage innovation and change in education and exploit it as an opportunity that addresses the needs of our students?

Developing a culture in which failures are accepted and innovation is encouraged will be difficult in the context of student learning where failures are frowned upon and excellence is expected. How can we use change models, strategies, and tools be used to be innovative and implement change?

The eighth commonality is the planning for a global future. For schools, the data is clear. There is a more diverse population in schools, lower socio-economic students, more English as a second language (ESL) learners, and more students graduating who are unprepared for the current and future job market. Teachers are often confused, disillusioned, and worried about their futures. Performance pay, evaluations tied to student achievement, and layoffs due to financial shortfalls are all taking their toll.

Teacher leaders need to help teachers plan for a global future. In developing such a plan teacher leaders need to recognize that certain barriers may preclude its success. For example, parents' work schedules, language difficulties for non-English speaking parents, and a lack of parent volunteers to interact with other parents may create difficulties. Obviously, careful consideration of any barriers should lead to alternatives to overcome them.

In other cases, the urgency for the change may be understood, where faculty and staff support is so strong that large-scale change can take place immediately. However, a pilot may be needed to convince staff a new reading program is effective for bilingual children. Perhaps the technology in a school may be so old that the entire staff embraces upgrading it and is eager to implement changes as soon as possible.

Obviously, changing the mechanisms by which services are delivered can be a daunting task. The essence of an organization is its culture. School systems seldom achieve anything significant without changing their values and overcoming the immutability of their culture. Change in schools needs to be transformative to be ready for a changing global marketplace.

SUMMARY

Schools are not static organizations. They are continually being challenged to change. The most recent challenge is the Common Core State Standards (CCSS) initiative. The future of public school education depends on a new paradigm that includes all levels of the organization—not just administrators with formal power. Teacher leaders can effect change within change.

Teacher leaders fill a number of roles in school systems, from department chairs to coaches and mentors. More and more research is pointing out the importance of teacher-led change whether it is formal or informal. There are many models for change within schools. Most of these theories talk about systemic change. Most systemic change in schools right now is a result of major federal and state drivers such as NCLB, CCSS, and state teacher evaluation legislation.

Teacher leaders are expected to be change agents for instruction improvement as well as coaches and mentors for teachers. They are involved in both *first-order* and *second-order* change but their primary focus must be on first-order change. This is the type of change that is grass roots, bottom up and results in incremental improvements in student learning.

Teacher leaders fulfill two coaching roles with regard to change. They are both content and change coaches. In order to be successful, they need specific leadership and pedagogical skills. The leadership skills provide a basis for developing *distributed leadership*. Pedagogical skills include the ability to promote collaboration, demonstrate, coach and mentor.

In the future, teacher leaders will face a number of challenges in the future. Tomal, Schilling, and Trybus (2013) refer to these as the *commonalities for change*. They include a human-centered school environment, desire to excel, business intelligence, sense of urgency, ed-entrepreneurship, impact of technology, incentivizing innovation, and planning for a global future.

Implementing change is a complex process that involves many variables. Those in formal power need to recognize the advantages of teacher-led change. Teacher leaders need to work within the system to effect incremental change that will not only improve student learning but will also lead to greater teacher satisfaction.

CASE STUDY

A Head Start for College

Every year, academically promising high school students in the Westin high school district fail to enroll in Advanced Placement (AP) courses. Most of these students are economically disadvantaged. Some of them do not know about these courses, while others assume they will be too difficult. Still others are held back by perceptions among teachers, whose referrals are often required for enrollment.

As a teacher leader in the social studies department at Westin High School, you notice that economically disadvantaged students are underrepresented in the AP courses in American and European history. You observe that a number of the teachers don't believe that these students can succeed in these classes. You decide to intervene.

In an effort to encourage more participation in AP American history classes, you meet with teachers in the department to discuss the matter. The teachers believe that they will need help in creating a new instructional model. They note that AP classes have been more like college classes. They rely on lectures, a fast pace to cover the entire material, and supportive home environment. They are concerned not only for the students but themselves.

As a teacher leader, you know that expanding access to the advanced classes can require far more effort on the part of teachers. You do some research and discover some strategies being used at other schools include tutoring at lunchtime, after school, and on Saturdays and allocating additional funds to pay for extra instructional time. Some schools are also offering study review classes.

Not all teachers in the department are happy with your initiative. They are concerned about what parents will think. They also worry that teachers will be forced to water down the curriculum. On the other hand, a small number of teachers don't see the benefit of including all students. They see little conclusive evidence that students who take AP courses perform better in college.

EXERCISES AND DISCUSSION QUESTIONS

1. Referring to the case study, how you would define the type of change needed? What would be the role of the teacher leader in implementing the change? What obstacles will the teacher leader face?
2. Referring to the case study, how could you use *shared leadership* to implement the change?
3. Referring to the case study, what leadership and change skills do you think the teacher leader will need?
4. Change initiatives often fail despite the best efforts of the leader. People's level of commitment and personal engagement are often determined by understanding why, how, and what the change is and what it means for them personally. Provide an example of resistance to change that you have experienced and analyze why it happened and what the leader could or should have done to deal with it.
5. Describe an example of a *first-order* and *second-order change* that has affected your professional life. Was the change implemented successfully? How did you feel about the change?

6. Pick one *commonalities for change* that will affect your school the most. How can the school and teacher prepare for the challenges it presents?
7. What should be the role of the principal, teacher leader, and teachers in implementing change?
8. Referring to the case study, what leadership and change skills do you think the teacher leader will need?
9. Identify a *teacherpreneur* in your school or have met. What makes him/her a teacherpreneur in your mind? What skill sets do they have that the average teacher does not?

REFERENCES

Berry, B., and TeacherSolutions 2030 Team (2011). *Teaching 2030: What we must do for our students and our public schools: now and in the future.* New York: Teachers College Press.

Daytona Beach News Journal (Oct 20, 2012). Scott sets expectations at the same level for all students. Retrieved from http://www.news-journalonline.com/article/20121020/OPINION/310199964

Evans, R. (1996). *The human side of school change.* San Francisco: Jossey Bass.

Fink, E., and Resnick, L. (2001, April). Developing principals as instructional leaders. *Phi Delta Kappan, 82,* 598–606.

McNeil, M. (Nov 16, 2012). Duncan sketches out second-term-agenda. *Education Week 1.* Retrieved from http://blogs.edweek.org/edweek/campaign-k-12/2012/11/Duncan_CCSSO_speech.html?intc=mvs

Rossi, R., Esposito, S., and Fitzpatrick, L. (Sep 18, 2012). Emanuel: deal is "honest compromise." *Chicago Sun Times.* Retrieved from http://www.suntimes.com/news/education/15224814-418/chicago-public-schools-teachers-strike-over.html

Senge, P. (1999). *The dance of change.* New York: Doubleday.

Stivers, J. and Cramer, S. (2009). *A teacher's guide to change.* Thousand Oaks, CA: Corwin.

Tomal, D., Schilling, C., and Trybus, M. (2013). *Leading school change: Maximizing resources for school improvement.* Lanham: Rowman & Littlefield Publishers, Inc.

Waters, T., Marzano, R. J., and McNulty, B. (2003). *Balanced leadership: What 30 years of research tells us about the effect of leadership on student achievement.* McREL (Mid-continent Research for Education and Learning).

Wynne, J. (2001). Teachers as leaders in education reform. *Eric Digest.* Retrieved from www.eric.ed.gov

Chapter 8

Managing Resources to Promote Student Learning

OBJECTIVES

At the conclusion of this chapter you will be able to:

1. Understand the role of teacher leaders in managing resources (ELCC 3.3, ISLLC 3, TLEC 2, 7, InTASC 2, 3, 10)
2. Describe the relationship between resources and achievement (ELCC 3.1, ISLLC 3, TLEC 2, 4, 7, InTASC 2, 3)
3. Articulate strategies for allocating resources for higher performance (ELCC 3.3, 4.3, ISLLC 3, 4, TLEC 2, InTASC 2, 3, 7)
4. Understand the concept of student-centric budgeting for allocating resources to improve student learning (ELCC 3.2, ISLLC 3, TLEC 1, 2, 5, InTASC 2, 3, 7, 9).
5. Describe the process for implementing and evaluating new initiatives (ELCC 3.2, ISLLC 3. TLEC 5, InTASC 2, 3, 7, 8)
6. Articulate the issues associated with procuring and managing technology in the classroom (ELCC 3.2, ISLLC 3, TLEC 2, InTASC 2, 3, 7)

RESOURCES AND STUDENT ACHIEVEMENT

According to the CCSS initiative, forty-five states have adopted the standards that focus on the core concepts each student needs to know at each grade level (Murphy and Regenstein, 2012). The establishment of standards is essential for targeting resources in the future. Clear standards should allow teacher leaders to allocate available resources more effectively at the classroom level.

As noted in earlier chapters, teacher leaders can assume several different roles: coach, mentor, and/or supervisor. Regardless of their role, however, teacher leaders must be part of the resource decisions in their schools to be effective. Teacher leaders who take on a traditional administrative role such as a department chairperson need to be familiar with basic resource allocation and budgeting procedures. Teacher leaders who take on more of a coaching role need to know where to procure and how to manage resources to assist teachers in improving student learning.

In school systems, the role assumed (administrator, supervisor, teacher leader, or teacher) sometimes brings a bias or perspective as to how resources should be used. For teacher leaders, the key question is, "Will allocating these resources make a difference in student achievement?" Textbox 8.1 illustrates some of the resource concerns for each level of leader.

What makes resource management especially difficult is the fact that there is not an overwhelming abundance of quality research that shows what works and what doesn't. Newstead, Saxton, and Colby (2008) assert that class size, an advanced college preparatory curriculum, teacher

TEXTBOX 8.1.
Resource Management Concerns for Educational Leaders

Leader	Focus	Resource Management Concerns
Superintendent District	• Local, state & federal funding • Community concerns • Fiscal sustainability • Compliance issues	• Procurement of adequate resources • Equity and distribution of resources by site • Monitoring and managing budgets
Principal Building	• Allocating funds • Compliance issues • Student performance	• Equity and distribution of resources within grade levels, departments, etc. • Student performance as defined by local, state and federal mandates
Teacher Leader Department	• Specific resources for subject, grade level or program • Classroom teacher support • Professional development	• Differentiated resources for teachers and students • Research • Professional development • Support for different teaching strategies • The tools of teaching—textbooks, technology, etc.

professional development, and differentiated instruction are key factors in helping all students learn. However, authors like Stephen Brill note that "if school systems stopped adhering to class size limits now that we know that class size counts less than the quality of the teacher in front of the class" (Brill, 2011).

Arnie Duncan, secretary of the Department of Education, also indicates the great importance of improving the quality of instruction. Providing students with high expectations begins with teachers being able to develop those high expectations as well as meeting them (Klein, 2009). Clearly, there are different philosophies on what matters the most.

From a teacher leader's perspective, the majority of the financial resources in schools should go toward supporting the instructional process, namely teachers and the tools for teaching. Everything else, in the strictest sense, supports the instructional process. Among other things, this would include professional development as well as coaching and mentoring of teachers. This is critical to the success of the teacher leaders as facilitators of student learning.

Just how much money is needed to make a difference is unknown. Hanushek and Lindseth (2009) found that the remedies in Kentucky, New Jersey, and Wyoming yielded virtually no change in patterns of achievement. Furthermore, Golab (2010) noted the following:

- Elementary students in Bannockburn had the fourth-highest test scores in Illinois last year, but that achievement wasn't reflected in the pay of their teachers, whose average salaries ranked 242nd among elementary school districts statewide.
- This north suburban school district is one example of the wide disparity between teacher pay and student achievement, which a *Chicago Sun-Times* analysis has found is common throughout Illinois.
- Just seven of the top twenty-five elementary districts with the highest-paid teachers also made the top twenty-five in student achievement scores.

What can be said, at best, is that the jury is out on the degree to which financial resources matter. Hanushek (1989) indicated that there was no strong relationship between school expenditures and student performance. Hedges, Laine, and Greenwald (1994) challenged that concept. They noted that financial resources do matter. In fact, to reach their conclusion, they relied on the same data most often used to demonstrate the opposite.

Hanushek (1986, 1989) examined data from thirty-eight different articles and books using regression coefficients to determine the effect of various inputs on student performance. Picus (1995) summarized his conclusions as follows:

- There was no conclusive statistical evidence that pupil-teacher ratio or teacher education resulted in increased student achievement.
- There was a positive correlation between teacher experience and salaries and student achievement. However, Hanushek (1989) noted that neither of these relationships was particularly strong.
- Per pupil expenditures were not a significant variable in determining student performance.
- Administrative inputs did not have a systematic relationship to student achievement and there was little relationship between the quality of school facilities and student performance.

Adams and Evans (2008) postulated that there are some inherent problems with the current way that finance systems target and link resources. They looked at five different attributes of financing systems: the resource target, the linkage between resources and educational programs, the resource management process, accountability, and the link between resources and student outcomes.

What Adams and Evans (2008) observed is that in conventional finance systems resources are directed toward district goals and there is no link between resources and education programs; spending is governed by categories; accountability is a matter of compliance; and the link between resources and outcomes is missing. In what they have termed Learning-Oriented Finance Systems, resources are targeted toward students, integrated with educational programs, and effectively used for continuous improvement; accountability is a function of student learning; and the link between resources and student outcomes is transparent (Adams and Evans, 2008).

In 2012, the Albert Shanker Institute issued a new report called *Revisiting the Age Old Question: Does Money Matter in Education?* (Baker, 2012). Baker basically looked at three questions:

1. Are the differences in aggregate school funding reflected in differences in short and long-term measured outcomes?
2. Are the differences in measured outcomes a result of differences in specific school programs and/or resources?
3. Does redistributing money or increasing the level of funding through state finance reforms lead to improvements in the distribution of student outcomes?

The answer to each question according to Baker is "yes." Baker noted that Hanushek's (1986) study has been the basis for the belief by many that money does not matter. He also noted that African American and other subgroup scores on the National Assessment of Educational Progress rose over time as school spending increased (Baker, 2012).

It is important to remember that educational resources include a broad spectrum of choices, from human resources to professional development to technology. Intuitively, we would all like to think more resources mean more learning. Unfortunately, a review of literature on the link between resources and achievement still creates more questions than answers. Even so, it is clear that the focus of the educational community is now clearly centered on student outcomes. This will inevitably lead to more discussion on how to align financial resources with student outcomes in the most productive and efficient manner. In order for this to happen, there will need to be a greater emphasis on data analysis and evaluation. Teacher leaders will be an integral part of this discussion.

ALLOCATING AND MANAGING RESOURCES

Teacher leaders are constantly challenged to assist teachers in meeting the academic and socializing goals for the students they educate. How do teacher leaders advocate for the allocation of resources to obtain those goals? Daggett (2009) notes that school districts need to focus "resources and accountability around specific tools, strategies, professional development, procedures, and policies that can be documented to improve student performance." He goes on to state that this is a subtle change from what currently exists. That is, it shifts the focus from inputs (programs) to outputs (student performance).

Teacher leaders need to incorporate strategies that help teachers improve their chances for success. It's not about the math or reading program. It's about Johnny's performance in reading or math. Consequently, resource allocation and budgeting decisions for the teacher leader should take a different approach.

Change is more likely to occur in budgeting systems where teacher leaders have control over human as well as financial resources and have the authority to make decisions about how they will be allocated. There are two types of change for which teacher leaders need to allocate funds. The first is a *pedagogical change,* such as would be typical in a routine curriculum review. The second is a *structural change,* such as changing class size standards. Furthermore, teacher leaders must address any continuing requirements to deliver the current program of studies.

Pedagogical change requires transition resources as well as implementation and evaluation resources for the proposed change. Transitional resources are one-time costs associated with planning and preparing for the change. Implementation resources are those costs associated with executing the change and include capital outlay, instructional materials, professional development and technology. Evaluation resources include the cost of technology to administer online tests, proctors, assessments, consultants, and other specialized services.

New courses, programs, and instructional strategies must contain a fiscal analysis or business plan. Teacher leaders must evaluate new initiatives from both an instructional and a fiscal basis, as well as determine if there is evidence that the results achieved are cost effective or whether the resources designated for the new initiative could be better spent on investing in current programs and services.

Often only the cost of staff and textbooks is examined. A better approach would be to include all costs: staff, benefits, professional development, supplies, textbooks, equipment, digital materials, facilities, and so on (see textbox 8.2). Some questions to ask are: "How many students will the initiative serve? Will there be a need for indirect resources such as counselors, media specialists, technologists, and others?

Public school districts have experimented with various forms of budget organization. *Line item and function/object budgeting* are basic to almost all systems. What varies from district-to-district and school-to-school is the methodology used to distribute resources through the budgeting and financial planning process (Cooper and Nisonoff, 2012).

TEXTBOX 8.2.
Sample Worksheet for New Initiatives

Initiative Name: *Reading Improvement Grades 1–3*

Number of Students Impacted: *130*   **Is this a Pilot Study: Y/N** N

Resource Requirements:	Salaries	Benefits	Supplies	Equipment	TOTAL
Staffing	45,000	4,000			49,000
Professional Development	7,500	750			8,250
New Textbooks			11,000		11,000
Tablet Computers				10,000	10,000
TOTAL	52,500	4,750	11,000	10,000	$78,250

Estimated Cost per Student	$602 per student
Are any of resources required being repurposed from other initiatives?	*Tablets from science*
Evaluation Methodology	*Growth in reading over next school year*
Definition of success (growth, score, % attaining competency, etc.	*5% improvement in students meeting state standards*

The purpose of prioritizing the budgeting process is to bring spending into alignment with policy priorities. It also eliminates repetition of services, establishes economies of scale, and creates parameters for downsizing. The point of allocating and budgeting resources is not to change for the sake of change. The goal of allocating and budgeting resources should be to assist teachers in implementing what the stakeholders in a district expect of their schools.

Regardless of what form of budgeting a school system uses, teacher leaders must have the authority to procure, allocate, and budget resources based on either research or results. In other words, it must be based on some type of evidence. Getting all stakeholders together to determine the distribution of funds within a program, department, or school requires not only a significant time commitment, but also knowledge of how resources impact student achievement.

The Student-Centric Budgeting Model (SCB) is an approach to educational resource allocation and budgeting that is based on identifying student needs and aligning resources to give teachers the tools they need to be successful (Schilling, 2013). This approach is extremely suited to teacher leader led change.

The central theme of this model is that teacher quality is the single most important ingredient in improving student achievement. Having teacher leaders who understand student needs and are able to quantify them for teachers is crucial for gains in student performance. A student-centric model would include the following strategies:

1. Understand what students need to achieve (data)
2. Find research supported approaches to meeting student needs (interventions)
3. Quantify what teachers need to meet student needs (resources)
4. Invest in strategies that return the greatest gains in student performance (efficiency)
5. Customize the strategies to the teacher (instruction)
6. Evaluate the success of the strategies (outcomes)

Collecting data to understand what students need to achieve is the first step in the student-concentric model. This involves mining the data, analyzing it and establishing action plans. The data needed will depend on the type of change desired: pedagogical or structural. Pedagogical change will most likely require standardized testing data. Structural change, such as adding staff, will most likely need to include other leadership.

The second step is finding *research-based interventions* to meet student needs based on the data analysis identified in step one. Interventions should be viewed from many possible perspectives. Interventions can be anything, from a simple change in a textbook, to pulling students out of the classroom for additional help. In either case, interventions require change from the status quo.

Quantifying the resources what teachers need to meet student needs is the third step. This involves establishing what resources are needed for teachers to be successful. Teacher leaders need to think in terms of differentiated instruction as opposed to system-wide programs. Teacher leaders are resource managers at the most basic level. If a teacher finds that students are failing to learn with one text, then they need to have the resources to provide a different book.

Determining what resources teachers need requires that teacher leaders be able to distinguish between individual and group needs. In either case, the key is to match resources with needs. This requires the cooperation of all teachers. This is about letting those closest to the instructional process set priorities and allocate funds.

Investing in efficient strategies that return the greatest gains in student performance is the fourth step. This seems simple but it is actually hard to do. This step requires assessment and research. For example, let's assume that a teacher leader has the following choice: he or she can implement a one-on-one technology strategy across the curriculum or add one additional teacher facilitator to each grade level. Which strategy is more effective? Which will generate the greatest gains in student achievement? How do teacher leaders arrive at the best decision?

Just as no two students learn in the same way, neither do teachers teach the same way. *Customizing instructional strategies* (step 5) to each teacher is critical for that teacher to be successful. Teacher leaders do this through the process of coaching and mentoring staff and providing them with the appropriate resources.

Evaluating the outcomes of the strategies selected is the final step in the process. Strategies that are unsuccessful or marginally unsuccessful should be reviewed to see if they are worth continuing. It is important to look at each step in the process. A breakdown in one step can lead to failures in others. Textbox 8.3 indicates the roles teacher leaders have for each step in the student-centric model.

Establishing a clear vision of what students need to succeed will promote sustainability and scalable success in student achievement over time. It is the first step to allocating resources. The natural inclination for most teacher leaders will be to address the most immediate needs of students and staff. This, of course, ignores planning for the long-term success. The goal of every teacher leader should be to provide equity over time and have a means of measuring it.

Developing criteria to ensure that test scores and student outcomes are met over time is crucial to allocating resources. This is especially impor-

TEXTBOX 8.3.
The Role of the Teacher Leader in the Student-Centric Model

Step	Role of the Teacher Leader
Data	Analyze and collect data that will clearly identify the interventions needed.
Interventions	Identify the interventions (or changes necessary) that will meet student needs.
Resources	Identify what resources teachers need to be successful.
Efficiency	Look for those strategies that will have the most impact.
Instruction	Customize instructional strategies to maximize individual teacher strengths.
Outcomes	Evaluate results for efficiency and success. Make a decision as to whether student needs have been met.

tant when protecting the needs of students from low-income families, English learners, and students with disabilities from the impact of budget cuts. The key to establishing broad goals is the involvement of all stakeholders in the process. Collaborative and meaningful engagement of all teachers is important to ensure the successful implementation of goals.

Each teacher leader needs to establish *financial parameters*. Financial parameters provide a basis for how funds are to be distributed, as well as benchmarks for measuring success. Teacher leaders should develop allocation recommendations based on teacher input and a review of the data. Teacher leaders are uniquely situated to know where resources are needed to achieve the goals of the school. Likewise, a significant portion of the resource allocation authority should reside with the teacher leaders and with the teachers with whom they collaborate.

Like most bureaucracies, schools and school districts tend to maintain programs already in existence and have difficulty eliminating those that are no longer effective. Demographics change as well as best practices and student needs. Confirming educational needs is an important role of the teacher leader. It forces the organization to reevaluate programs in light of student outcomes. The result of such a process is that resources can be reallocated and realigned to promote student achievement in a more productive and efficient manner.

Teacher leaders need to ensure compliance with all legal requirements. Most categorical programs such as special education, Response to Intervention (RTI), and bilingual programs have specific requirements set by the state. RTI, which focuses on research-based interventions and instruction for general education students, has been adopted by a growing number of states (Zirkel, 2011). With its focus primarily on reading improvement, RTI may hold the promise of reducing costs by implementing early interventions.

There are several strategies to confirm an organization's current instructional needs. Among these is reviewing information that will shed light on which practices, programs, and policies have been effective and produced measurable improvements in student achievement and/or outcomes. Simply put, invest in what works. This is especially important in times of limited educational resources. Shifting resources from less effective to more effective programs and strategies will most likely result in the greatest benefits for students. To achieve effectiveness, teacher leaders must have data systems from which to draw evidence and conclusions.

MANAGING TECHNOLOGY

The New Media Consortium, the Consortium for School Networking and the International Society for Technology in Education released their findings regarding the near, mid- and long-term impact of technology on K–12 education (Johnson et al., 2013). The report indicated that in the short-term mobile technologies and cloud computing would have the biggest impact. There is already a move toward tablets and other mobile devices due to their price point and ease of use. Cloud computing reduces the cost of technology infrastructure for school districts.

Regarding the midterm, the report sees learning analytics and open content as having the most impact. Learning analytics refers to being able to use technology to analyze and prescribe resources to meet individual student needs. The open-content movement in K–12 has already started. Some examples of open content software include the following:

- Firefox: Internet and security software
- Audacity: Audio editor and recorder
- Gimp: High-end graphics software

For the long-term, the reports speculate that 3-D printing and virtual laboratories will change the way teachers demonstrate concepts and scientific experiences. 3-D printing is simply being able to print (make) a three-dimensional object. Virtual labs will allow students access to an array of experiments using desktop virtualization that can take place in the classroom or at home. Virtual labs can also be customized based on the ability and performance of the student.

If these are some possible trends in technology in schools, what are the implications for allocating resources? Along with teacher interventions, technology will be used to power student learning in the future. It will be used to do the following:

- Assess student achievement, goals, and resource allocation
- Track resources spent on each student, class, school, etc., to determine their effectiveness as well as the effectiveness of the prescribed academic interventions
- Analyze the strengths of teachers and match them to students and schools
- Collect data on every student
- Allow more equitable access to educational opportunities by increasing student, staff and parent access to the curriculum and other resources

Technology can play a significant role in increasing productivity at every level of the education system. Teacher leaders can utilize open-sourced software, digital textbooks, online delivery systems, and other technology-based resources that can provide low-cost and up-to-date materials.

*Open-sourced softw*are is available without charge to organizations. A good example of open source web software is Moodle, a Course Management System (CMS) or Virtual Learning Environment (VLE). Moodle is used by school districts to augment face-to-face courses as well as to deliver online instruction. Moodle allows users to copy, use, and modify the software under certain conditions.

Open-source software is an important development in the K–12 educational community (see textbox 8.4). It has the potential to save money. It

TEXTBOX 8.4.
Open-source Resources

Open-source Resources	*Website*
Guide to the Use of Open Educational Resources in K–12 and Postsecondary Education (2013)	go.nmc.org/guideopen
Open Resources: Transforming the Way Knowledge is Spread (2012)	go.nmc.org/opener
If You Like Learning, Could I Recommend Analytics? (2013)	go.nmc.org/elit
Enhancing Teaching and Learning Through Data Mining and Learning Analytics: An Issue Brief (2012)	go.nmc.org/enh
"Opening" a New Kind of School: The Story of the Open High School of Utah (2013)	go.nmc.org/openew
Survey on Governments' Open Educational Resources Policies (2012)	go.nmc.org/surv

can also be freely shared with all students and be can be customized for specific needs.

Digital materials such as textbooks can be used to provide additional online learning programs for students, can be modified to meet a variety of student and teacher needs, and can create new opportunities for students in rural areas. Of course, teacher leaders need to be cognizant of ensuring that all students have access to the technology.

The primary purpose of technology should be to support the instructional process. Technology decisions and costs should be part of any planning for new initiatives or changes to the curriculum. For teacher leaders the first question that needs to be answered is, "What value will the proposed technology add to student learning?" The second question is, "Where do you want to be in the technology continuum?"

In addressing the first question, teacher leaders can draw on library media specialists as well as technology specialists. School library media specialists are instructional partners, as well as information specialists (School Library Media Coordinator Program, 2010). They can serve as coaches to introduce, model, instruct, and support teachers in the use of technology to enhance student learning (Harvey, 2011).

For example, media specialists can teach students using Hyper Studio while simultaneously modeling for teachers (Harvey, 2011). They can also recommend specific technology tools for teachers to use such as Scratch, Minecraft, and Tynker for math to meet CCSS (American Association of School Librarians, Achieve, 2013).

Library media specialists are also in a unique position to facilitate cooperative, interdisciplinary teaching using technology (American Association of School Librarians, Achieve, 2013). Cooperative teaching is two or more teachers collaborating to teach a subject. A school librarian, for example, might collaborate with both history and language arts teachers to teach students how to use Google Site to create primary source documents for a study on the *Gettysburg Address* (American Association of School Librarians, Achieve, 2013).

The technology continuum includes technology that is both tried and tested as well as technology that has been newly introduced in the market. The problem with buying only "tried and tested" technology is the speed at which it changes. Holding onto old technology is no better than hanging onto old textbooks unless there is some overriding value in doing so.

The future of technology in the classroom is networked based. Common Core testing is already making demands on network bandwidth. The use of *one-to-one* computing devices including tablets, chrome books, and laptops is becoming a common instructional strategy. For teacher leaders making the digital leap, one of the greatest obstacles can be figuring out how to show teachers how to manage the tech-infused classroom.

Some questions that are often asked are: How do you keep students on the Internet safe? How do you maintain the technology? How do you involve all teachers—those technologically challenged as well as the most tech-savvy? Teachers face a wide array of student abilities, learning styles, interests, knowledge, and levels of motivation. Teacher leaders need the skills to address increasingly challenging classroom dynamics, as well as differences in student abilities.

SUMMARY

Whether teacher leaders are managers in the traditional sense or coaches and mentors, they need to understand the role that resources play in supporting student learning. School districts, and consequently teacher leaders, are continually being challenged to do more with less. The 2008 economic downturn only exacerbated that fact. In order to obtain higher performance, teacher leaders need to ensure that resources are being allocated to where they make the most impact, while being mindful to maintain intra-district equity for various groups within the district.

It is imperative that teacher leaders understand the relationship between resources and student achievement from an empirical basis. If educational resources, including staff, money, and/or time, are going to be committed, then there should be evidence that they are effective.

The CCSS initiative is the latest approach to improve student learning in the United States. For it to be successful, teacher leaders will need to have the authority to target resources as well as to redirect them as they discover what works.

Technology is rapidly changing the face of teaching. Technology presents additional problems for the classroom teacher as well as for the teacher leader. It is almost unreasonable to believe that individual teachers will be able to keep up with all the technological change especially when they are being asked to do more research-based instruction. The teacher leader can fill that role. While they may not know everything, teacher leaders are in a unique position to assist teachers in finding the resources they need and that are effective.

The future of public school education in the United States is dependent on improved instructional strategies that are not only efficient, but also effective. Finding more productive and effective means for obtaining educational outcomes (which have basically evolved to standardized tests) is the challenge for teacher leaders.

The need for teacher leadership in the allocation of resources will become even more crucial with the implementation of Common Core standards. Teacher leaders, although not managers, impact the use of staff, money and time in order to increase student achievement. It is incumbent on teacher leaders to demonstrate that "money matters." To do that, they need to find what works.

CASE STUDY

Aligning Student Outcomes with Educational Resources

Smallville Unified School District (SUSD) is a diverse K–12 system located in a suburban setting next to a large urban city. You are a teacher leader working with all of the fourth and fifth grade teachers in the district. You have looked at the performance data for fourth and fifth grade students and found that one of the greatest needs is to improve the reading scores of these students.

SUSD is currently considering allocating resources to purchase portable tablets through Title 1 funding. Approximately 40 percent of the school's student population falls within the definition of low income. You are aware of several studies that have shown that portable tablets used in the classroom can increase reading test scores. The data show that the district has not made annual yearly progress (AYP) for the last three years.

After talking to some parents, you note that there are families that do not have adequate reading materials or even newspapers at home for the students to read. The school district has funded a number of initiatives. These include professional development programs, the lowering of class sizes, adding new positions (such as counselors, gifted, and special education teachers) as well as receiving grants (reading, math, social emotional learning, and technology).

All students in the fourth and fifth grades have been identified because did they did not make the target of 85 percent proficiency in either math or reading. You have been working to improve the school's academic program by offering professional development to teachers in the areas of reading and mathematics for all students.

EXERCISES AND DISCUSSION QUESTIONS

1. Referring to the case study, indicate how you could use the student-centric model in budgeting resources in your district.
2. Referring to the case study, write two-to-three paragraphs on what data you would collect and what strategies you would employ in order to implement procuring portable tablets for classrooms.

3. In the school system where you currently work or reside, how are resource allocation decisions determined? Is there a process for teacher input?
4. What should be the role of teacher leaders in allocating resources and evaluating their effectiveness? Is there a difference in the role of grade level teacher leaders as opposed to teacher leaders who are coaching and mentoring a department?
5. What is the difference between effectiveness and efficiency? Provide an example of a change that was effective but not efficient, and a change that was not effective but efficient.
6. From your perspective, what are the challenges of implementing and managing technology in the classroom? Where does technology fall in the continuum of resources that need to be funded?
7. What are the pros and cons of giving teacher leaders more control over a school's operating budget? Is improving student performance easier to obtain when teacher leaders have control of all the resources for their school?
8. Pick an initiative with which you are familiar that has failed. Why was it not successful? Is there anything that could have been done to make the change successful?

REFERENCES

Adams, J. E., and Evans, D. J. (2008). *Funding student learning: How to align education resources with student learning goals.* National Working Group on Funding Student Learning. Seattle: University of Washington, Center on Reinventing Public Education.

American Association of School Librarians, Achieve. (2013, October 31). *Implementing the Common Core State Standards: The Role of the School Librarian.* American Library Association. Retrieved December 15, 2013, from Achieve.org: http://www.ala.org/aasl/sites/ala.org.aasl/files/content/externalrelations/CCSSLibrariansBrief_FINAL.pdf

Baker, B. D. (2012). *Revisiting the age-old question: does money matter in education?* Washington, DC: Albert Shanker Institute.

Brill, S. (2011). *Class warfare: inside the fight to fix america's schools.* New York: Simon & Schuster.

Cooper, B., and Nisonoff, P. (2012). *Public school budgeting, accounting, and auditing.* May 15. www.encyclopedia.com/doc/1G2-3403200507.html.

Daggett, W. (2009, April). *Effectiveness and efficiency framework—a guide to focusing on student performance.* Retrieved from leadered.com: http://www.leadered.com/pdf/EE%20%20White%20Paper%20website%203.25.09.pdf

Golab, A. (2010, April 19). High teacher pay no guarantee of results. *Chicago Sun-Times.* Retrieved from HighBeam Research: http://www.highbeam.com/doc/1N1-12F31B7FE4BB7140.html

Hanushek, E. (1986). The economics of schooling: Production and efficiency in public schools. *Journal of Economic Literature* 24:1141–77.

———. (1989). The impact of differential expenditures on school performance. *Educational Researcher 18*(4): 45–65.

Hanushek, E. and Lindseth, A. (2009) Schoolhouses, courthouses, and statehouses: solving the funding-achievement puzzle in America's public schools. Princeton: Princeton University Press.

Harvey, C. A. (2011, October). The Coach in the Library. *Educational Leadership, 69*(2). Retrieved December 15, 2013, from http://www.ascd.org/publications/educational-leadership/oct11/vol69/num02/The-Coach-in-the-Library.aspx

Hedges, L. V., Laine, R. D., and Greenwald, R. (1994). Does money matter? A meta-analysis of studies of the effects of differential school iinputs on student outcomes. *Educational Researcher, 23*(3), 5–14.

Johnson, L., Adams Becker, S., Cummins, M., Estrada V., Freeman, A. and Ludgate, H. (2013). NMC Horizon Report: 2013 K-12 Edition. Austin, TX: The New Media Consortium.

Klein, A. (2009 January 13). Nothing but praise for Duncan in senate hearing. *Education Week.* www.edweek.org/login.html?source=http://www.edweek.org/ew/articles/2009/01/13/18duncan.h28.html&destination=http://www.edweek.org/ew/articles/2009/01/13/ 18duncan.h28.html&levelId=2100.

Murphy, P. and Regenstein, E. (2012). *Putting a price tag on the common core: How much will smart implementation cost?* Washington, DC: Thomas Fordham Institute.

Newstead, B., Saxton, A., and Colby, S. (2008, June 6). Going for the gold: Secrets of successful schools. *Education Next, 8*(2): 38–45.

Picus, L. O. (1995). *Does money matter in education?* Retrieved from National Center for Education Statistics: http://nces.ed.gov/pubs97/web/97536-2.asp

Schilling, C. A. (2013). The school business official as a change agent. Boston: ASBO International Presentation.

School Library Media Coordinator Program. (2010). Retrieved from The University of North Carolina at Chapel Hill: http://sils.unc.edu/programs/slmc

Scott sets expectations at the same level for all students. (2012, October 20). *Daytona Beach News Journal.* Retrieved from http://www.news-journalonline.com/article/20121020/OPINION/310199964

Zirkel, P. A. (2011). State laws and guidelines for RTI: Additional implementation features. *Communique, 39*(7). Retrieved from National Association of School Psychologists: http://www.nasponline.org/publications/cq/39/7/professional-practice-state-laws.aspx

Chapter 9

School Improvement and Teacher Leadership

OBJECTIVES

At the conclusion of this chapter you will be able to:

1. Understand the school improvement process and the steps in creating a school improvement plan (ELCC 1, 2, 3, 4, 5, ISLLC 1, 2 4, 5, TLEC 1, 2, 4, 5, InTASC 1, 2, 3, 6, 7, 8, 10)
2. Articulate the models for improving low performing schools (ELCC 1, 2, 3, 4, 5, ISLLC 2, 3, 4, 5, TLEC 1, 2, 4, 6, InTASC 1, 2, 3, 6, 7, 8, 10)
3. Recognize the role and importance of teacher leaders in the school improvement process (ELCC 2, 3, ISLLC 1, 2, 4, 6, TLEC 3, 4, 5, 6, InTASC 8, 9, 10)
4. Describe the critical issues in promoting school improvement (ELCC 2, 3, 4, 5, ISLLC 3, 4, 5, 6, TLEC 1, 2, 3, 5, 6, InTASC 7, 8, 9, 10)
5. Understand the five factors necessary to improve *professional capacity* (ELCC 2, 3, 4, ISLLC 2, 3, 6, TLEC 2, 3, 4, 6, InTASC 5, 6, 7, 8, 9, 10)
6. Identify the key components to establishing and obtaining accountability (ELCC 2, 3, 4, 5, ISLLC 2, 3, 5, TLEC 5, 6, InTASC 1, 2, 6, 7, 8, 9, 10)

MODELS FOR SCHOOL IMPROVEMENT

Ever since *A Nation at Risk* (1983), educators have been testing strategies to improve schools for both academic and social purposes. Over thirty years later, we are still testing strategies. We have invented *small learn-*

ing communities, professional learning communities, block scheduling, the CCSS initiative, science, technology, engineering, and mathematics (STEM), and *school improvement plans* (SIP) to name a few. We have disaggregated data: low income, at-risk, special education, ESL, and ethnicity. Finally, we have attempted to improve schools legislatively through such laws as NCLB and RTTT. Along with local efforts, these are but a few of the attempts that have been made to reform education.

A growing body of research says that teacher quality matters. What we don't know is how money, class size, and other resources impact student learning. Consequently, states are mandating changes in professional training for both administrators and teachers. Illinois recently changed its entire principal preparation program. It now requires every principal to take and pass teacher evaluation training as part of the curriculum. Up to fifty percent of teachers', as well as principals', evaluations are based on student performance. Other states have taken similar measures as a result of NCLB and RTTT.

Teacher leaders need to play a key role in improving student learning and teacher quality. In order to maximize their success, however, teacher leader roles in school improvement will have to change. Enculturation of these changes will have to take place. Teacher leader responsibilities will need to continue to evolve from "administrative" to "coach and mentor."

School Improvement

State departments of education typically provide templates for school improvement planning (SIP). These plans are not, however, models for school improvement. They are prescriptive plans to comply with state and federal directives. They are plans for improving instruction when schools fail to meet some minimum measures such as a standardized test, outcome, or other measurement.

Typically, a school improvement plan is required when an individual school or school district fails to meet some minimum requirement. The plan must address the achievement of all students. Data must be disaggregated and reviewed to see that all groups of students are achieving. This would include a breakdown by gender, racial and ethnic groups, special education, English language learners, and socioeconomic status.

School improvement plans are approved by boards of education and the state. Compliance monitoring is done by the state. Plans are required to be updated every year until such time as compliance is obtained. In Ohio, the state has created what is referred to as the *Ohio Improvement Process* (OIP) *Guide*. As noted in the OIP, the objective is not to simply comply with state and federal requirements but to improve education for every student in every school.

The aim of the OIP is to produce locally high-achieving schools. The guide recommends a five-stage process (Ohio Department of Education, 2012):

- Stage 0: Preparing for the OIP
- Stage 1: Identifying Critical Needs
- Stage 2: Developing a Focused Plan
- Stage 3: Implementing and Monitoring the Focused Plan
- Stage 4: Evaluating the Improvement Process

The OIP process is predicated on seven guiding principles. Those guiding principles can be summarized as follows:

1. Every step in the process should be aligned to the vision, mission, and philosophy.
2. The plan should be based on the concept of continuous improvement. Continuous improvement simply means a cycle of continuous evaluation, implementation, and re-evaluation.
3. The basis for the plan is sound research and data analysis.
4. The community and other stakeholders such as students, parents, and teachers should provide input and collaborate on the plan.
5. There should be ongoing communication with the community regarding issues and their insights.
6. The plan should be all-inclusive. There should be one integrated plan that reflects Title I, special education, ESL, career and technical education, and any other requirements.
7. The plan has high expectations for all participants. This means that there is an expectation that both students and teachers will improve in some significant way.

The OIP includes in its definition of leadership, teacher leaders from content areas, grade levels, buildings, and special instructional areas such as gifted, special education, and so on. The goal of the OIP is to create a framework for continuous planning and improvement. While the process may seem cumbersome and complex, it is designed to focus efforts and improve learning (Ohio Department of Education, 2012).

Federally Mandated Intervention Models

In 2010 President Obama noted that 12 percent of the nation's schools produce about 50 percent of its dropouts. Secretary of Education Duncan noted that the U.S. Department of Education was targeting five thousand of the lowest performing schools by providing them Title I School Improvement Grants (Terry, 2010).

Under the Title I School Improvement Grant program, states must identify their lowest performing schools in economically challenged areas and use one of four models to improve student achievement in those schools. The four models include (1) turnaround, (2) restart, (3) school closure, and (4) transformation. The most popular model is transformation. Not everyone is in agreement that these four models adequately address all situations. It would be difficult, for example, to use a restart or closure model in a rural town where there is only one high school. Additionally, there are concerns on finding the right model for each school.

Turnaround model: The turnaround model requires that all staff be released. A new principal is hired who has substantial site-based authority to hire staff, allocate resources, and so on. Under this model up to 50 percent of the previous staff can be rehired. Under this model a school might introduce new instructional methods, implement an instructional data analysis system, and/or develop a teacher performance system based on student achievement.

Restart model: The restart model requires the school be closed and reopened under the operation of a charter school operator, a charter management organization, or an education management organization that has been selected through a rigorous review process. Restarts have the greatest potential to impact student achievement quickly. This is because a third-party operator can bring in a new staff, culture and proven techniques to improve student achievement.

School closure model: Under the school closure model, the school is permanently closed and the students are enrolled in other schools in the district that are higher achieving. This option can generate savings that can be reinvested where students of the closed schools are relocated. The success of this model is entirely dependent on the ability of the district to move students to higher performing schools.

Transformation model: The transformation model is the most popular of the four options. Under this model, the school must implement the following strategies: (1) replace the principal and take steps to increase teacher and school leader effectiveness, (2) institute comprehensive instructional reforms, (3) increase learning time and create community-oriented schools, and (4) provide operational flexibility and sustained support.

Benwood Schools in Chattanooga, Tennessee, is an example of a transformation school. The initiatives introduced included teacher evaluation, teacher coaching, leadership and professional development, and merit pay plans. Transformations are not generally considered to have as dramatic effects as the other models.

Reform Models

There is not one reform model that works for all schools. School reform is something that is extremely difficult, if not impossible, without support from the school district. District policies need to be aligned to support the right expectations and programmatic reforms to make higher objectives reachable. The National Governors Association (NGA) created set of recommendations for state policymakers to consider in turning around low-performing schools. The governors suggested the following five strategies be considered to improve schools (National Governors Association Center for Best Practices, 2003):

1. Align standards and assessments with the expectation that all students need to be ready for college success.
2. Increase student and teacher supports, including sustained professional development and time for collaborative efforts.
3. Ensure adequate human and financial resources to meet the scope and degree of educational challenges faced by the schools.
4. Create small, focused high schools that prepare all students for the future.
5. Support robust, high-quality public school choice options.

The NGA was also the architect of the CCSS initiative along with the CCSSO. The standards were developed with the input of teachers, administrators, and experts. Feedback from national organizations representing community college and university educators, civil rights groups, and protected classes of students, among others.

These Common Core standards define the knowledge and skills students should acquire during their K–12 education that will allow them to succeed in entry-level, credit-bearing academic college courses and in workforce training programs (National Governors Association Center for Best Practices, 2010). The criteria as noted by the NGA and CCSSO in their "Introduction to the Common Core State Standards" dated June 2, 2010 is as follows:

- Are aligned with college and work expectations.
- Are clear, understandable and consistent.
- Include rigorous content and application of knowledge through high-order skills.
- Build upon strengths and lessons of current state standards.
- Are informed by other top performing countries, so that all students are prepared to succeed in a global economy and society.
- Are evidence-based.

CRITICAL ISSUES IN PROMOTING SCHOOL IMPROVEMENT

The *classroom* and *school* are important intervention points for improving student achievement. What critical factors distinguish successful schools from those less successful schools in implementing school improvement? What is the role of teacher leaders in promoting school improvement success?

While no two schools are alike, there are a number of common issues that can be critical to their success. These factors, along with others, constantly shape school improvement. They include the following:

- Enculturation
- Structure vs. instruction
- Professional capacity
- Fiscal resources
- Community outreach and support
- Site-based management

Enculturation

Gruenert (2008) notes that *school climate* reflects the attitudes and perceptions of groups. It impacts all stakeholders, especially teacher leaders, teachers and students. "How students, teachers, and staff feel about their school climate underlies individual attitudes, behaviors, and group norms" (Loukas, 2007, p. 1).

The role of teacher leaders with respect to climate has changed over the years. Silva, Gimbert, and Nolan (2000) identified *three waves* of teacher leader roles. In the first wave, teacher leaders were typically seen as administrators. In the second wave, they were primarily instructional experts: curriculum, mentors, and professional development. The third wave, however, is what they refer to as "reculturing" schools. This requires that teacher leaders initiate changes in culture to promote collaboration and a continuous improvement.

To shape school culture, teacher leaders need to help teachers establish a positive school climate. Since change is part of the school improvement process, it is important to establish a climate in which staff feels connected. As a result, staff will be more unified and focused on improving student learning and achievement. According to Lortie (1975), the amount of effort a teacher will make is related to the degree to which the teacher perceives that effort will make a difference. The impact of intrinsic rewards cannot be overstated.

How any school improvement model is implemented is one of the most important factors to its success. When there is a shared vision among staff, and teachers are active participants in the school improvement plan, implementation and improvements will be more successful. When the reform is imposed upon the school by the district or by the principal, improvements will not be as readily seen. Just having a strong vision and prescribing a solution will not engender buy-in and a shared vision to improve instruction.

Structure versus Instruction

Kauffman (1999) observed that "if we are going to help students . . . we are going to have to change course. We cannot continue to avoid focusing on instruction! We cannot continue to suppose that consultation and collaboration will somehow make up for the deficit in instruction." The focus of most initiatives before NCLB was on changing the structure of education. In fact, some would argue that it is still the focus.

Adopting a block schedule, changing from a junior high school to a middle school model, implementing small learning communities in a high school or introducing professional learning communities are all attempts at changing education structurally. These attempts are directed at the way schools are organized in order to increase student learning and achievement. Unfortunately, by themselves, these changes have not attained in the kinds of growth in learning and achievement desired.

In recent years, the emphasis has shifted towards teacher quality and student outcomes. This shift has significant implications for teacher leaders. Their roles reflect a gradual shift from structural leadership (department chairs and administrators) to instructional leadership (coaches and mentors). CCSS, NCLB, and other initiatives are all designed to improve the quality of instruction.

Professional Capacity

One of the most important roles of teacher leaders is to increase the professional capacity. The assumption is that improving the professional capacity of teachers will result not only in a better climate but an improved learning environment. Professional capacity is not dependent on any one model or reform. It is essential for all models and/or reforms to succeed.

Professional capacity can be determined by reviewing a number of environmental factors among others. These factors would include the following:

1. Collaboration among staff
2. Resourcefulness and ingenuity among teachers
3. The presence of enhanced instructional practices

4. Formal and informal professional development opportunities present
5. The overall professional status of teachers

The presence, or lack thereof, of these factors should give teacher leaders a perspective on the overall capacity of the staff they are working with and what they may need to do to improve it.

Fiscal Resources

Every school needs adequate fiscal resources for the successful implementation of reform. Teacher leaders can use supplemental funding from state and federal grants, where appropriate, to provide additional funding for training and consultants. Furthermore, to successfully implement some changes, a considerably larger staff of teachers and instructional aides is necessary, as well as adequate space.

Funding from the local school foundation may be possible to fund some teacher-led initiatives. Teacher leaders can play an active role in grant writing by teachers to obtain additional funding. They can assist the principal in lobbing the school district for extra resources to help with start-up costs for new programs.

To successfully make changes, it is likely that teacher leaders will need to use multiple strategies and resources. For example, funding for professional development and training may come from Title I, new classroom technology from the district foundation and the start-up costs for textbooks and materials from the school district.

Community Outreach and Support

Teacher leaders can enlist the help of social workers and other interventionists to successfully involve community businesses and agencies. Linking students and their families to the resources offered by these businesses and agencies can provide everything from eye exams and clothing to tutoring and summer jobs. In addition to links with community businesses and agencies, teachers themselves can serve as important resources for parents. Teachers should be expected to have regular contact with their students' parents (see table 9.1). Teachers can involve parents in after-school activities and invite them to work with them.

The importance of community support is also important. Positive relationships with local businesses and agencies such as church groups can be an important focus. A parent coordinator to build relationships with parents and to increase parent involvement may be an option. A parent resource room with computers managed by a parent coordinator could offer parents serve as a learning resource for both students and parents.

Table 9.1. Sample Standards of Parental Involvement

Standard	Involvement
Communication	Communication between home and school is regular, two-way and meaningful
Parenting	Parenting skills are promoted and supported
Student learning at home	Parents play an integral role in assisting student learning
Volunteering	Parents are welcome in the schools and their support and assistance is sought
School decision-making	Parents are full partners in the decisions that affect children and families
Collaborating with the community	Community resources are used to improve schools, families and student learning

A parent outreach component can serve two major purposes. First, it can serve to increase parental involvement with the school and with their children's learning. Secondly, it can provide assistance to children when health or home problems interfere with their academic performance (see table 9.2).

Site-Based Management Reform

Site-based management (SBM) is an effort to allow schools to tailor programs to meet their individual needs. SBM allows the development of a holistic approach to address the academic and personal needs of students and of their families. It can also encourage the formation of strong relationships with community businesses and outreach organizations.

Table 9.2. Sample Action Plan for Parental Involvement

Critical Element	Action/Activity	Who is Responsible	Start Date	Project Finish	Date to be evaluated?
1	A welcoming environment	All staff	After training	Ongoing	Each meeting and year end
2	Programs to engage family in student learning	School leadership team	After leadership team talks	Ongoing	Each meeting and year end
3	Establish strong teacher-family relationship	Teachers	By the end of October	Ongoing	Monthly
4	Family interactive skill professional development with school staff	School leadership team and PTA	Immediately after PTA is established	Ongoing	After each PTA meeting and year end

Effective SBM reform also advances collaboration by involving multiple stakeholders in the school improvement process, including the principal, teacher leader, teachers, parents, and community members. The key drawback of SBM is that it is difficult to replicate at other schools. It is tailored to meet the specific needs of a particular school and it is difficult, if not impossible, to replicate and transport it other schools.

The success of SBM is also highly dependent on the effectiveness of the leadership at the school. If the principal, teacher leader, or teachers do not provide a strong vision for improvement that is embraced by all, then improvement efforts are unlikely to work. A related drawback is that each school must "reinvent the wheel."

ESTABLISHING AND OBTAINING ACCOUNTABILITY

Data analysis and information can assist teacher leaders adjust learning strategies and professional development to changing conditions and lessons learned as change is introduced. Periodic program evaluations to gather information about strategies and program activities and results serve many purposes including evaluating program strategy, internal accountability, creating compliance, and community accountability.

Evaluating program strategy. Evaluation helps determine whether the strategies that are being used to achieve the desired outcomes are working. Results of evaluations are used as a basis for identifying problem areas and making changes to improve overall effectiveness. Most change models start and end with data collection and evaluation as a means for continuous program improvement.

Internal accountability. Periodic evaluations of success provide a basis for establishing a system to hold everyone accountable for the implementation and effectiveness of the program. Establishing an accountability system involves defining performance goals, obtaining commitments from people to achieve those goals, and evaluating their performance against those goals. Where necessary, action(s) may be necessary to improve performance. Accountability is valuable to teacher leaders to ensure the quality of the program at all levels

Creating compliance. Periodic reporting of program activities and successes contributes to compliance by raising awareness. Staff wants to be part of a successful activity. On the other hand, if the program is not being successful, there is a good chance that nonconformance will occur. When that happens, the teacher leader needs to identify the issues and respond to them.

Community accountability. In most states, schools are required by law to report their progress and achievements to the public. Program evaluation provides the basis for community accountability. This accountability can be an important force in shaping program strategies and priorities. Schools may be required to do improvement plans, for example, as a result of not meeting minimum state and federal benchmarks for student learning and performance.

Accountability ensures quality. Teacher leaders need to clearly establish expectations, obtain commitments from their staffs, measure performance and reward success. Success can be measured through a number of variables including student achievement, student outcomes, and/or instructional outcomes.

SUMMARY

Teacher leaders play an integral role in school improvement. They fill an important leadership role in implementing reform models to increase student achievement, improving classroom instruction, and creating a professional teaching climate. As long as the focus continues to be on teacher quality, teacher leader roles will continue to grow.

The SIPs are generally prescriptive plans developed by state departments of education. They are formal plans that must be approved by boards of education and state boards of education. Generally, the plans include data analysis, the identification of critical needs, a plan for implementation and monitoring, and an evaluation component.

Under Title I, there are four models for improving the lowest performing schools. The models include turnaround, restart, closure, and transformation. Turnaround requires all staff and the principal be released and a new principal and no more than 50 percent of the staff be rehired. The restart model requires that a third party take over the school. The closure model requires that the school be closed and the students are reassigned to higher performing school.

The most popular model is transformation. Under this model the school must replace its principal as well as institute instructional reforms, increase learning time and community-oriented schools, and provide more operational flexibility to the school.

In addition to SIPs and Title I models, there are other reform models. These reform models tackle the issue of low performing schools from an array of perspectives. The NGA has set forth a number of recommendations regarding strategies to improve schools. The NGA is also the architect, along with the CCSSO, in creating the CCSS initiative (National Governors Association Center for Best Practices, 2010).

There are a number of critical factors in promoting school improvement. They include enculturation, structure versus. instruction, professional capacity, fiscal resources, community outreach and support and site-based management reform. Each of these factors is critical to the success of schools. Teacher leaders have evolved from administrators to instructional experts and now to "reculturing."

Evaluating program strategy, internal accountability, creating compliance, and community accountability are essential to establishing and maintaining overall accountability for school improvement plans. Data analysis and information provide teacher leaders with the tools to adjust learning strategies and professional development to changing conditions.

CASE STUDY

Nova Middle School (NMS) is, by many measures, successful in educating students. The schools' current year School Improvement Plan states:

It should be noted that on the Department of Education Report Card we were rated in the upper end of satisfactory. Our achievement index score was rated satisfactory with a score of 73.8 (a score of 75.0 or higher is considered outstanding). Our attendance rating was considered outstanding showing further improvement from the previous year. Our student participation rating for taking exams was also considered outstanding. We tested 99.2 to 100 percent of all students. (current year SIP)

While NMS may be on the upper end of satisfactory, there is room for improvement among its subgroup populations. Data from state and antidotal sources indicate areas in which academic achievement needs to be improved. Surveys and anecdotal data indicate other areas in which the school needs to improve—primarily in closing the achievement gap and attendance for the subgroups, which include limited English proficient, students with disabilities, Hispanic, and other nonwhite subgroups.

NMS currently has forty-one licensed staff members (including specialists and administrators) with a student-teacher ratio of 25:1. The average years of teacher experience is 12.3, and 85.4 percent of all teachers have a master's degree. NMS serves students in grades 6, 7, and 8. Student enrollment in last year was 815. The current enrollment is around 830. Of that number, 37.1 percent received free or reduced lunch and 5.8 percent speak English as a second language. Ethnicity is reflected in figure 9.1 and the number of years of teaching experience is reflected in figure 9.2.

Student attendance at NMS is 94.7 percent and testing participation is 99.2 percent. The school has fewer expulsions and behavior referrals than any other middle school in the district the past two years. The state rates the school's achievement as satisfactory and their attendance and participation rate as outstanding. School performance data over a combined two-year period is shown in table 9.3. Table 9.4 shows the

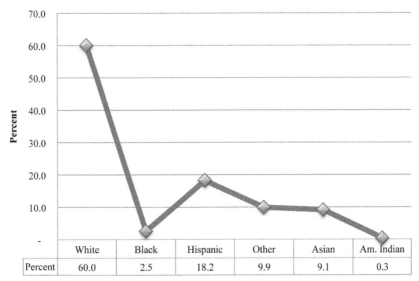

Figure 9.1. Ethnic Distribution of Nova Middle School

	White	Black	Hispanic	Other	Asian	Am. Indian
Percent	60.0	2.5	18.2	9.9	9.1	0.3

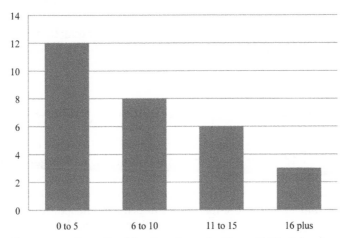

Figure 9.2. Years Teaching Experience for Nova Middle School

Table 9.3. Nova Middle School Performance Data

School Performance Data		
	Reading	Math
% Meets	47.3	37.8
% Exceeds	30.2	38.5
% Meets or Exceeds	77.5	76.3
% Meets, Exceeds, or Meets Growth	82.5	82.1

Table 9.4.   Nova Middle School Subgroup Performance Data

Subgroup Performance Data		
Reading—Academic Status		
Students	% Met	Growth Change
All Students	77.49	4.01
Limited English Proficient	41.41	–0.6
Students with Disabilities	39.41	–0.6
Math—Academic Status		
All Students	76.26	–0.1
Limited English Proficient	46.70	–1.29
Students with Disabilities	42.37	–3.13
Hispanic	49.24	–0.72

subgroup performance in the academic areas of reading and math is significantly below the all students group.

The Leadership Team composed of a counselor, dean of students, two teacher leaders and the principal, meet weekly. At every meeting, the team reviews data to note updates and discuss further actions to be taken. By tracking and analyzing data, they have been able to identify trends in behavior, absenteeism, and grades based on racial or cultural subgroups.

EXERCISES AND DISCUSSION QUESTIONS

1. Referring to the case study, as a teacher leader what recommendations would you make to the leadership team with regard to closing the differences in achievement between the subgroups and overall school population? Explain how you would integrate the *Common Core Standards* into the instructional program based on a data.
2. Referring to the case study Nova, Middle School has decided to create a parent action-plan. As a teacher leader what would be your role? How would you involve the teaching staff? How would you involve parents and/or community members?
3. Identify one goal at your school that has not been successful. Why was it unsuccessful? How would you build a culture that might create "staff buy-in" for the change (i.e., team building, consensus building, and brainstorming)?
4. Describe the components of a school improvement plan in your state, and how these components should be created to bring about successful change. Analyze your own school improvement plan and explain how it was developed, implemented, and assessed.

5. Review the data reported to the state and public about your school (i.e., school report card or and any other data used by the school/organization for improvement). Analyze your data to determine the strengths and weakness of the school. Identify three major needs based on your data collection, and three positive aspects or strengths of your school/organization.

6. Interview your building principal to discuss her/his perspective on the role of the teacher leader in the school improvement process. Discuss the "vision" of the school and the principal's expectation of how teacher leaders support it.

7. Interview a community member (parent, board member, alum, local resident, business owner, etc.) to understand their perception of the school. Based on their perceptions, determine several ways to collaborate with the community and involve them in decision making. Discuss how the culture and climate of the school/organization help or hinder change and improvement.

8. Research national, state, and local compliance initiatives that most schools are required to address and how you would explain them to faculty resulting in tangible outcomes.

REFERENCES

A Nation at Risk (1983). Retrieved from http://www.scribd.com/doc/49151492/

A-Nation-at-Risk Common Core Standards Initiative (2012). Retrieved from http://www.corestandards.org/

Gruenert, S. (2008). School culture, school climate: They are not the same thing. *Principal, 87*, (4), 56–59. Retrieved from http://www.naesp.org/resources/2/Principal/2008/M-Ap56.pdf

Jorgensen, M. and Hoffman, J. (2003). *History of the No Child Left Behind Act (NCLB).* Retrieved from http://www.pearsonassessments.com/NR/rdonlyres/D8E33AAE-BED1-4743-98A1-BDF4D49D7274/0/HistoryofNCLB.pdf.

Kauffman, J. (1999). "Commentary: Today's special education and its message for tomorrow." *Journal of Special Education, 32*(4), p. 244–254.

Lortie, D. (1975). *Schoolteacher: A sociological study.* Chicago: The University of Chicago Press.

Loukas, A. (2007). What is school climate? *Leadership Compass, 5*(1), 1–3. Retrieved from http://www.naesp.org/resources/2/Leadership_Compass/2007/LC2007v5n1a4.pdf

National Governors Association Center for Best Practices. (2003). *Reaching new heights: Turning around low-performing schools.* Retrieved from http://www.nga.org/files/live/sites/NGA/files/pdf/0803REACHING.pdf

National Governors Association Center for Best Practices, Council of Chief State School Officers. (2010). *Common Core State Standards:* Retrieved from National

Governors Association Center for Best Practices, Council of Chief State School Officers, Washington, DC. website: http://www.corestandards.org/the-standards

Ohio Department of Education (2012). *Ohio improvement process (OIP) guide: Facilitating districtwide improvement in instructional practices and student performance.* Retrieved from http://education.ohio.gov/getattachment/Topics/School-Improvement/Transforming-Schools/Ohio-Improvement-Process-OIP-Resources-2012/Complete-OIP-Guide.pdf.aspx

Silva, D. Y., Gimbert, B., and Nolan, J. (2000). Sliding the doors: Locking and unlocking possibilities for teacher leadership. *Teachers College Record, 102,* 779–804, cited in York-Barr, J., and Duke, K. (2004). What do we know about teacher leadership? Findings from two decades of scholarship. *Review of Educational Research, 74*(3), 255–316.

Stivers, J. and Cramer, S. (2009). *A teacher's guide to change.* California: Corwin.

Terry. D. (2010). Retrieved from http://www.ed.gov/blog/2010/03/whats-possible-turning-around-americas-lowest-achieving-schools/

Appendix A

Teacher Leader Websites

2020 Forecast: Creating the Future of Learning
   http://futureofed.org/wp-content/uploads/2011/07/2020-Forecast.pdf
Annenberg institute
   http://annenberginstitute.org/
Association of School Business Officials International (ASBOI)
   http://www.asbointl.org
Association for Supervision and Curriculum Development (ASCD)
   www.ascd.org
Center for Comprehensive School Reform
   http://www.centerforcsri.org
Center for Safe Schools
   http://www.safeschools.info/emergency-management
The change leader
   http://www.cdl.org/resource-library/articles/change_ldr.php
Closing the achievement gaps
   http://www.edtrust.org/dc/press-room/press-release/states-can-close-the
   -achievement-gap-by-decades-end-new-education-trust-
Council of Chief State School Officers
   http://www.corestandards.org/the-standards
Department of Labor Summary of Major Laws
   www.dol.gov/opa/aboutdol/law
Education Commission of the States
   http://www.ecs.org
Education leadership improves student learning
   http://www.wallacefoundation.org/knowledge-center/school-leadership/
   Pages/default.aspx
ELCC Standards of the NPBEA (National Policy Board for Educational Administration)

http://suu.edu/ed/pdf/elddstandards.pdf
Equal Employment Opportunity Commission Laws and Statutes
http://www.eeoc.gov/laws/statutes/index.cfm
Great Schools by Design
http://www.archfoundation.org/category/featured-programs/great-schools-by-design/
Leading change
http://www.educationalleaders.govt.nz/Leading-change
Leading change from the classroom: Teachers as leaders
https://www.sedl.org/change/issues/issues44.html
National Center for Educational Statistics (NCES)
http://nces.ed.gov
National Clearinghouse for Educational Facilities
http://www.ncef.org
National Conference of State Legislatures (NCSL)
http://www.ncsl.org
National Educational Technology Standards for Administrators
http:// www.iste.org, iste@iste.org
National Governors Association Center for Best Practices
http://www.nga.org
No Child Left Behind
http://www.ed.gov/nclb/
Ohio Department of Education
http://education.ohio.gov
Race-to-the-Top
http://www2.ed.gov/policy/gen/leg/recovery/statutory/stabilization-fund.pdf
School Improvement Grants
http://www.ed.gov/category/program/school-improvement-grants
Teacher and leader effectiveness
http://www.doe.k12.ga.us/School-Improvement/Teacher-and-Leader-Effectiveness/Pages/default.aspx
Teacher leader model standards
http://teacherleaderstandards.org/
Teacher leader voice and capacity building lead to student growth
http://www.edwardsedservices.com/teacher-leader-voice-and-capacity-building-lead-to-student-growth/
U.S. Department of Agriculture, Food and Nutrition Service, National School Lunch Program
http://www.fns.usda.gov/cnd/Lunch/AboutLunch/ProgramHistory_4.htm
U.S. Department of Education
http://www.ed.gov
U.S. Department of Labor Occupation Safety and Health Administration (OSHA)
http://www.osha.gov/
U.S. Environmental Protection Agency, Healthy School Environments (EPA)
http://www.epa.gov/schools/

Appendix B

Teacher Leader Model Standards

DOMAIN I

Fostering a Collaborative Culture to Support Educator Development and Student Learning

The teacher leader understands the principles of adult learning and knows how to develop a collaborative culture of collective responsibility in the school. The teacher leader uses this knowledge to promote an environment of collegiality, trust, and respect that focuses on continuous improvement in instruction and student learning.

DOMAIN II

Accessing and Using Research to Improve Practice and Student Learning

The teacher leader understands the evolving nature of teaching and learning, the established and emerging technologies, and school community. Uses this knowledge to promote, design, and facilitate job-embedded professional learning aligned with school improvement goals.

DOMAIN III

Promoting Professional Learning for Continuous Improvement

The teacher leader understands the evolving nature of teaching and learning, established and emerging technologies, and the school community. The teacher leader uses this knowledge to promote, design, and facilitate job-embedded professional learning aligned with school improvement goals.

DOMAIN IV

Facilitating Improvements in Instruction and Student Learning

The teacher leader demonstrates a deep understanding of the teaching and learning processes and uses this knowledge to advance the professional skills of colleagues by being a continuous learner and modeling reflective practice based on student results. The teacher leader works collaboratively with colleagues to ensure instructional practices are aligned to a shared vision, mission, and goals.

DOMAIN V

Promoting the Use of Assessments and Data for School and District Improvement

The teacher leader is knowledgeable about current research on classroom- and school-based data and the design and selection of appropriate formative and summative assessment methods. The teacher leader shares this knowledge and collaborates with colleagues to use assessment and other data to make informed decisions that improve learning for all students and to inform school and district improvement strategies.

DOMAIN VI

Improving Outreach and Collaboration with Families and Community

The teacher leader understands that families, cultures, and communities have a significant impact on educational processes and student learning. The teacher leader works with colleagues to promote ongoing systematic collaboration with families, community members, business and community leaders, and other stakeholders to improve the educational system and expand opportunities for student learning.

DOMAIN VII

Advocating for Student Learning and the Profession

The teacher leader understands how educational policy is made at the local, state, and national level as well as the roles of school leaders, boards of education, legislators, and other stakeholders in formulating those policies. The teacher leader uses this knowledge to advocate for student needs and for practices that support effective teaching and increase student learning, and serves as an individual of influence and respect within the school, community, and profession.

Source: The Teacher Leadership Exploratory Consortium, 2010

Appendix C

Technology Standards for School Administrators

I. **Leadership and Vision**—Educational leaders inspire a shared vision for comprehensive integration of technology and foster an environment and culture conducive to the realization of that vision.

Educational leaders:
   A. Facilitate the shared development by all stakeholders of a vision for technology use and widely communicate that vision
   B. Maintain an inclusive and cohesive process to develop, implement, and monitor a dynamic, long-range, and systemic technology plan to achieve the vision
   C. Foster and nurture a culture of responsible risk-taking and advocate policies promoting continuous innovation with technology
   D. Use data in making leadership decisions
   E. Advocate for research-based effective practices in the use of technology
   F. Advocate on the state and national levels for policies, programs, and funding opportunities that support implementation of the district technology plan

II. **Learning and Teaching**—Educational leaders ensure that curricular design, instructional strategies, and learning environments integrate appropriate technologies to maximize learning and teaching.

Educational leaders:
   A. Identify, use, evaluate, and promote appropriate technologies to enhance and support instruction and standards-based curriculum leading to high levels of student achievement

B.   Facilitate and support collaborative technology-enriched learning environments conducive to innovation for improved learning

C.   Provide for learner-centered environments that use technology to meet the individual and diverse needs of learners

D.   Facilitate the use of technologies to support and enhance instructional methods that develop higher-level thinking, decision making, and problem-solving skills

E.   Provide for and ensure that faculty and staff take advantage of quality professional learning opportunities for improved learning and teaching with technology

III. **Productivity and Professional Practice**—Educational leaders apply technology to enhance their professional practice and to increase their own productivity and that of others.

Educational leaders:

A.   Model the routine, intentional, and effective use of technology

B.   Employ technology for communication and collaboration among colleagues, staff, parents, students, and the larger community

C.   Create and participate in learning communities that stimulate, nurture, and support faculty and staff in using technology for improved productivity

D.   Engage in sustained, job-related professional learning using technology resources

E.   Maintain awareness of emerging technologies and their potential uses in education

F.   Use technology to advance organizational improvement

IV. **Support, Management, and Operations**—Educational leaders ensure the integration of technology to support productive systems for learning and administration.

Educational leaders:

A.   Develop, implement, and monitor policies and guidelines to ensure compatibility of technologies

B.   Implement and use integrated technology-based management and operations systems

C.   Allocate financial and human resources to ensure complete and sustained implementation of the technology plan

D.   Integrate strategic plans, technology plans, and other improvement plans and policies to align efforts and leverage resources

E.   Implement procedures to drive continuous improvement of technology systems and to support technology replacement cycles

V. Assessment and Evaluation—Educational leaders use technology to plan and implement comprehensive systems of effective assessment and evaluation.

Educational leaders:
  A. Use multiple methods to assess and evaluate appropriate uses of technology resources for learning, communication, and productivity
  B. Use technology to collect and analyze data, interpret results, and communicate findings to improve instructional practice and student learning
  C. Assess staff knowledge, skills, and performance in using technology and use results to facilitate quality professional development and to inform personnel decisions
  D. Use technology to assess, evaluate, and manage administrative and operational systems

VI. Social, Legal, and Ethical Issues—Educational leaders understand the social, legal, and ethical issues related to technology, and model responsible decision making related to these issues.

Educational leaders:
  A. Ensure equity of access to technology resources that enable and empower all learners and educators
  B. Identify, communicate, model, and enforce social, legal, and ethical practices to promote responsible use of technology
  C. Promote and enforce privacy, security, and online safety related to the use of technology
  D. Promote and enforce environmentally safe and healthy practices in the use of technology
  E. Participate in the development of policies that clearly enforce copyright law and assign ownership of intellectual property developed with district resources

Source: These standards are the property of the TSSA Collaborative and may not be altered without written permission. The following notice must accompany reproduction of these standards: "This material was originally produced as a project of the Technology Standards for School Administrators Collaborative." Foundation Standards Developed by the TSSA Collaborative Draft v4.0 4 Draft Date 11/5/01

Appendix D

ISLLC Leadership Standards

Standard 1: An education leader promotes the success of every student by facilitating the development, articulation, implementation, and stewardship of a vision of learning that is shared and supported by all stakeholders.

A. Collaboratively develop and implement a shared vision and mission
B. Collect and use data to identify goals, assess organizational effectiveness, and promote organizational learning
C. Create and implement plans to achieve goals
D. Promote continuous and sustainable improvement
E. Monitor and evaluate progress and revise plans

Standard 2: An education leader promotes the success of every student by advocating, nurturing, and sustaining a school culture and instructional program conducive to student learning and staff professional growth.

A. Nurture and sustain a culture of collaboration, trust, learning, and high expectations
B. Create a comprehensive, rigorous, and coherent curricular program
C. Create a personalized and motivating learning environment for students
D. Supervise instruction
E. Develop assessment and accountability systems to monitor student progress
F. Develop the instructional and leadership capacity of staff
G. Maximize time spent on quality instruction

H. Promote the use of the most effective and appropriate technologies to support teaching and learning
I. Monitor and evaluate the impact of the instructional program

Standard 3: An education leader promotes the success of every student by ensuring management of the organization, operation, and resources for a safe, efficient, and effective learning environment.

A. Monitor and evaluate the management and operational systems
B. Obtain, allocate, align, and efficiently utilize human, fiscal, and technological resources
C. Promote and protect the welfare and safety of students and staff
D. Develop the capacity for distributed leadership
E. Ensure teacher and organizational time is focused to support quality instruction and student learning

Standard 4: An education leader promotes the success of every student by collaborating with faculty and community members, responding to diverse community interests and needs, and mobilizing community resources.

A. Collect and analyze data and information pertinent to the educational environment
B. Promote understanding, appreciation, and use of the community's diverse cultural, social, and intellectual resources
C. Build and sustain positive relationships with families and caregivers
D. Build and sustain productive relationships with community partners

Standard 5: An education leader promotes the success of every student by acting with integrity, fairness, and in an ethical manner.

A. Ensure a system of accountability for every student's academic and social success
B. Model principles of self-awareness, reflective practice, transparency, and ethical behavior
C. Safeguard the values of democracy, equity, and diversity
D. Consider and evaluate the potential moral and legal consequences of decision making
E. Promote social justice and ensure that individual student needs inform all aspects of schooling

Standard 6: An education leader promotes the success of every student by understanding, responding to, and influencing the political, social, economic, legal, and cultural context.

  A. Advocate for children, families, and caregivers
  B. Act to influence local, district, state, and national decisions affecting student learning
  C. Assess, analyze, and anticipate emerging trends and initiatives in order to adapt leadership strategies

Source: *The ISLLC Standards.* Interstate School Leaders Licensure, Consortium of Chief State School Officers, 2011.

Appendix E
ELCC Standards

Standard 1.0: Candidates who complete the program are educational leaders who have the knowledge and ability to promote the success of all students by facilitating the development, articulation, implementation, and stewardship of a school or district vision of learning supported by the school community.

Elements	Indicators
1.1 Develop School District Vision	a. Develop a school/district vision b. Base vision on relevant theory
1.2 Articulate Vision	a. Articulate components of vision b. Use data-based research strategies to inform vision c. Communicate school/district vision
1.3 Implement Vision	a. Formulate initiatives to motivate staff, students, and families b. Plans for implementation of school/district vision
1.4 Steward Vision	a. Understanding role of effective communication skills to build shared commitment b. Design system for using data-based research strategies c. Assume stewardship of school/district vision
1.5 Promote Community Involvement	a. Involve community members in realization of vision b. Communicate effectively with all stakeholders in implementation

Standard 2.0: Candidates who complete the program are educational leaders who have the knowledge and ability to promote the success of

all students promoting a positive school culture, providing an effective instructional program, applying best practice to student learning, and designing comprehensive professional growth plans for staff.

Elements	Indicators
2.1 Promote Positive School Culture	Assess school culture using multiple methods and strategies

2.2
Provide Effective
  Instructional
  Program
	a. Apply principles of effective instruction to improve instructional practices
	b. Design curriculum to accommodate diverse learner needs
	c. Use technology to enrich curriculum and instruction

2.3
Apply Best
  Practice
  to Student
  Learning
	a. Assist school personnel to apply best practices for student learning
	b. Apply human developmental, learning, and motivational theories to learning process
	c. Use research strategies to promote environment for improved student achievement

2.4
Design
  Comprehensive
  Professional
  Growth Plans
	a. Implement well-planned professional development programs
	b. Use observation, collaborative reflection, adult learning strategies to form professional growth plans with teachers and school personnel
	c. Develop and implement personal professional growth plans that reflect a commitment to life-long learning

Standard 3.0: Candidates who complete the program are educational leaders who have the knowledge and ability to promote the success of all students by managing the organization, operations, and resources in a way that promotes a safe, efficient, and effective learning environment.

Elements	Indicators
3.1 Manage the Organization	a. Optimize the learning environment by applying appropriate models of organizational management b. Develop plans of action for focusing on effective organization and management of fiscal, human, and material resources c. Manage time effectively and deploy financial and human resources in ways to promote student achievement
3.2 Manage Operations	a. Involve staff in conducting operations and setting priorities using needs assessment, research-based data, and group process skills to build consensus b. Develop communications plans for staff to develop family and community collaboration skills c. Understand how to apply legal principles

Elements	Indicators
3.3 Manage Resources	a. Use problem-solving skills and knowledge of strategic long-range and operational planning in use of fiscal, human, and material resource allocation b. Creatively seek new resources to facilitate learning c. Apply and assess current technology for school management, business procedures, and scheduling

Standard 4.0: Candidates who complete the program are educational leaders who have the knowledge and ability to promote the success of all students by collaborating with families and other community members, responding to diverse community interests and needs, and mobilizing community resources.

Elements	Indicators
4.1 Collaborate with Families and the Community	a. Bring together family and community resources to positively affect student learning b. Involve families in the education of their children c. Use public information and research-based knowledge to collaborate with families and the community d. Create frameworks for school, family, business, community, government, and higher education partnerships using community-relations models e. Develop various methods of outreach aimed at business, religious, political, and service organizations f. Involve families and other stakeholders in school decision-making processes g. Demonstrate the ability to collaborate with community agencies to integrate health social, and other services h. Develop a comprehensive program of community relations and demonstrate ability to work with the media
4.2 Respond to Community Interests and Needs	a. Demonstrate active involvement within the community including persons with conflicting perspectives b. Use appropriate assessment strategies and research methods to accommodate diverse school and community conditions c. Provide leadership to programs serving students with special and exceptional needs d. Capitalize on the diversity of the school community to improve school programs and meet diverse student needs
4.3 Mobilize Community Resources	a. Use community resources including youth services to support student achievement, solve problems, and achieve school goals b. Use school resources and social service agencies to serve the community c. Demonstrate ways to use public resources and funds appropriately to encourage communities to provide new resources to address student problems

Standard 5.0: Candidates who complete the program are educational leaders who have the knowledge and ability to promote the success of all students by acting with integrity, fairly, and in an ethical manner.

Elements	Indicators
5.1 Acts with Integrity	a. Demonstrate a respect for the rights of others with regard to confidentiality, dignity, and engage in honest communications.
5.2 Acts Fairly	a. Combine impartiality, sensitivity to student diversity, and ethical considerations in interactions with others.
5.3 Acts Ethically	a. Makes and explain decisions based on ethical and legal principles.

Standard 6.0: Candidates who complete the program are educational leaders who have the knowledge and ability to promote the success of all students by understanding, responding to, and influencing the larger political, social, economic, legal, and cultural context.

Elements	Indicators
6.1 Understand the Larger Context	a. Act as informed consumers of educational theory and concepts and apply appropriate research methods to a school context b. Explain how legal and political systems and institutional framework of schools shape a school and community c. Analyze the complex causes of poverty and their effects on families, communities, children, and learning d. Understand school policies, laws, and regulations enacted by local, state, and federal authorities e. Describe the economic factors shaping a local community and economic factors affecting schools f. Analyze and describe the cultural diversity in a school community g. Describe community norms and values and how they relate to the role of the school in promoting social justice h. Explain various theories of change and conflict resolution
6.2 Respond to the Larger Contest	a. Communicate with members of a school community concerning trends, issues, and potential changes in the school environment and maintain ongoing dialogues with diverse community groups
6.3 Influence the Larger Context	a. Engage students, parents, and the community in advocating the adoption of improved policies and laws b. Apply understanding of larger context to develop activities and policies that benefit students and their families c. Advocate for policies and programs that promote equitable learning opportunities and success for all students

Standard 7.0: Internship. The internship provides significant opportunities for candidates to synthesize and apply the knowledge and practice and develop the skills identified in Standards 1–6 through substantial, sustained, standards-based work in real settings, planned and guided cooperatively by the institution and school district personnel for graduate credit.

Source: *ELCC Standards*, Educational Leadership Consortium Council (ELCC), 2002.

Appendix F

Interstate Teacher Assessment and Support Consortium (InTASC)

Model Core Teaching Standards

Standard 1: Learner Development—The teacher understands how learners grow and develop, recognizing that patterns of learning and development vary individually within and across the cognitive, linguistic, social, emotional, and physical areas, and designs and implements developmentally appropriate and challenging learning experiences.

Standard 2: Learning Differences—The teacher uses understanding of individual differences and diverse cultures and communities to ensure inclusive learning environments that enable each learner to meet high standards.

Standard 3: Learning Environments—The teacher works with others to create environments that support individual and collaborative learning and that encourage positive social interaction, active engagement in learning, and self-motivation.

Standard 4: Content Knowledge—The teacher understands the central concepts, tools of inquiry, and structures of the discipline(s) he or she teaches and creates learning experiences that make these aspects of the discipline accessible and meaningful for learners to assure mastery of the content.

Standard 5: Application of Content—The teacher understands how to connect concepts and use differing perspectives to engage learners in critical thinking, creativity, and collaborative problem solving related to authentic local and global issues.

Standard 6: Assessment—The teacher understands and uses multiple methods of assessment to engage learners in their own growth, to monitor learner progress, and to guide the teacher's and learner's decision making.

Standard 7: Planning for Instruction—The teacher plans instruction that supports every student in meeting rigorous learning goals by drawing upon knowledge of content areas, curriculum, cross-disciplinary skills, and pedagogy, as well as knowledge of learners and the community context.

Standard 8: Instructional Strategies—The teacher understands and uses a variety of instructional strategies to encourage learners to develop deep understanding of content areas and their connections and to build skills to apply knowledge in meaningful ways.

Standard 9: Professional Learning and Ethical Practice—The teacher engages in ongoing professional learning and uses evidence to continually evaluate his or her practice, particularly the effects of his of her choices and actions on others (learners, families, other professionals, and the community), and adapts practice to meet the needs of each learner.

Standard 10: Leadership and Collaboration—The teacher seeks appropriate leadership roles and opportunities to take responsibility for student learning, to collaborate with learners, families, colleagues, other school professionals, and community members to ensure learner growth, and to advance the profession.

Source: Council of Chief State School Officers. (2011, April). Interstate Teacher Assessment and Support Consortium (InTASC) Model Core Teaching Standards: A Resource for State Dialogue.

Index

About the Authors

Daniel R. Tomal, PhD, is a Distinguished Professor of Leadership at Concordia University Chicago teaching in the educational leadership and doctoral programs. He has been a public school teacher, administrator, consultant, and corporate vice president. He is author of fifteen books, including *Action Research for Educators* (a CHOICE Outstanding Academic Title), *Managing Human Resources and Collective Bargaining*, and *Resource Management for School Administrators* (with Craig Schilling), and *Leading School Change* (with Marge Trybus and Craig Schilling) by Rowman & Littlefield Education, and has made guest appearances on many national radio and television shows such as CBS *This Morning*, NBC *Cover to Cover*, ABC News, *Les Brown*, *Joan Rivers*, and *Chicago Talks*.

Craig Schilling is an associate professor of Educational Leadership at Concordia University Chicago, River Forest, IL. He has been a public school administrator, systems analyst, and CEO. He has consulted from numerous school districts and has spoken and presented at over one hundred workshops and training seminars throughout the United States, Canada, and the Caribbean. He is coauthor of the books *School Resource Management: Optimizing Fiscal, Facilities, and Human Resources* (with Dan Tomal), *Human Resource Management and Collective Bargaining* (with Dan Tomal), and *Leading School Change* (with Marge Trybus and Dan Tomal), all published by Rowman and Littlefield.

Robert K. Wilhite is a professor at Concordia University Chicago and chair of the Department of Educational Leadership. He is a former elementary, middle school, and high school principal, associate superintendent for curriculum and instruction, and superintendent of schools. He has published several articles and made extensive presentations at conferences across the United States in the areas of intervention programs for homeless students, adaptive leadership styles for the twenty-first century, and technology integration and curriculum development. He also currently serves on the Illinois Licensure Board, Principal Review Panel, evaluating the design of university principal preparation programs in Illinois.

9 781475 807455